Exophony

Also by Yoko Tawada

Yoko Tawada

Exophony
Voyages Outside the Mother Tongue

translated from the Japanese by Lisa Hofmann-Kuroda
introduced by Naoise Dolan

dialogue
books

First published in the United States in 2025 by New Directions
First published in Great Britain in 2025 by Dialogue Books,
an imprint of John Murray Press

SRD

Originally published in Japanese as *Ekusofoni: Bogo No Soto E Deru Tabi*.
Published by arrangement with Iwanami Shoten, Tokyo.

Grateful acknowledgement is made for lines by Paul Celan, quoted
from *Memory Rose into Threshold Speech* and translated by Pierre Joris
(Farrar, Straus & Giroux); Basho, quoted from *Narrow Road to the Interior*
and translated by Nobuyuki Yuasa (Penguin); and Jack Spicer, quoted
from *After Lorca* (New York Review of Books Poets).

A CIP catalogue record for this title is available from the British Library

Trade Paperback ISBN 978-0-349-70419-7
ebook ISBN 978-0-349-70418-0

Printed and bound in India by Manipal Technologies Limited, Manipal

John Murray policy is to use papers that are natural, renewable and
recyclable products and made from wood grown in sustainable forests.
The logging and manufacturing processes are expected to conform to
the environmental regulations of the country of origin.

Carmelite House
50 Victoria Embankment
London EC4Y 0DZ

MIX
Paper | Supporting
responsible forestry
FSC
www.fsc.org   FSC™ C104740

www.dialoguebooks.co.uk

John Murray Press, part of Hodder & Stoughton Limited
An Hachette UK company

Contents

Preface

THROUGH LANGUAGE, THE WORLD IS IN CONSTANT
motion. Trying to grasp that motion in its totality would be
like trying to catch every species of fish in the sea at the same
time—impossible, in other words. At first, I tried using terms like
"immigrant literature," "border crossing," "creole," "minority,"
"translation" as my net, hoping to catch a few schools of fish that
way, but I didn't get very far. So instead, I decided to become a
fish myself and swim around to all the different oceans in the
world. As a frequent traveler, I soon realized that writing this way
suited me best. I could suddenly express all that I wanted to say.
And that's how the names of cities came to replace the series of
abstract nouns that had previously occupied *Exophony*'s chapter
headings. Fish that I am, I used my scales to feel out the linguistic
textures of each place as I went swim-walking about. And it was
through these sensations—illuminating and being illuminated
by all that I had read, thought, and heard—that this book slowly
and steadily took shape.

YOKO TAWADA

Introduction

I READ *EXOPHONY* ON TOUR IN MILAN AND LIGURIA, doing interviews and a literary event in my sixth language, Italian. Something in me comes alive in Italian, like a champagne bottle popping spontaneously. It's the most ad hoc of the languages I've learned—no formal study, no extended time in the country, gleaned mainly from novels and podcasts—and I have fun in it. Indeed, I'd just written my first few articles in Italian. The day I arrived in Milan I bought *La Stampa* at a kiosk near the central station to read my own words in print. I didn't have cash so, in an ironically consumerist twist, I impulse-bought a book on *capitalismo di guerra* (war capitalism) to meet the card minimum.

Twice on this trip journalists asked me if I would ever write fiction in any of my languages besides English. The first time I answered unequivocally that I would not; I wrote the odd thing privately in other languages as an exercise but none of them could rival the stylistic control I enjoy in English. By the next time I was posed the question, I had finished reading Yoko Tawada's take on the matter and had changed my mind. I'm the boss in English, but maybe it's more interesting not to be. Authority isn't everything.

Tawada's is not a show-off polyglot manifesto. She writes in her native Japanese and in German, and the ambiguities and dissonances between the two interest her more than any conventional display of linguistic virtuosity. 'I'm not interested in studying lots of languages', she says frankly. 'To me, it's the space between languages that's most important, more than the languages themselves. Maybe what I really want is not to be a writer of this or that language in particular, but to fall into the poetic ravine between them.'

Over the course of this delightful essay collection, Tawada navigates this lacuna with wit and wonder. She does not speak solely to the language freaks—guilty as charged—but to anyone curious about words. Her understanding of exophonic literature is not an actuarial calculation of how many languages a writer speaks, but how flexible they are on the page. Paul Celan, who wrote only in German, is spiritually a multilingual poet for Tawada: his knowledge of French and Russian seeps through in moments like his punning of the visually identical *Neige* (neglect) with the French *neige* (snow). I speak French and German and had never thought to make the connection because the words sound so different. On her tour through the ravine, Tawada stops to re-examine what you thought you already knew.

Native English speakers will come away from this book better acquainted with their mother tongue. Tawada's discussion of anglicisms in other languages reveals what is distinct and worth borrowing in our own. She charts this influence in detail, from the lavishing of English loanwords on Japanese adverts to the rise in German word-for-word calques like 'Das macht Sinn', a hyper-literal translation of 'That makes sense'. A middle-aged German once praised me for saying 'Das ergibt Sinn', lamenting that not all native speakers my age still did. Tawada does not share such speakers' judgement. She is inquisitive about trends, honest about finding some innovations ugly but willing to accept that languages change.

Sometimes the rupture is the point. In 'Spelling Words' Tawada explores how the uncertainty of a foreign tongue can free one intellectually and artistically. 'So long as I'm writing in Japanese', she says, 'the impulse to avoid certain taboo subjects is automatically activated. When I write in other languages, however, this function goes dormant. I find myself being bolder and expressing things I would never have thought to say otherwise.'

To Tawada, languages are not private property and native speakers do not hold the deeds. She enjoys listening to French without understanding a word of it; she flips through a German thesaurus as if window-shopping. In speaking a foreign language, you can trust your own instinct: 'If you dislike a word, there is always some reason for it, even if you cannot explain it immediately, and it is usually tied to your personal memories and aesthetics'. The non-native speaker is not a humble supplicant but a poet and innovator. '[L]osing your accent isn't the goal of learning a language', Tawada insists.

With this joy in multilingualism, she holds a simultaneous awareness that it is often the result of oppression. Here she is in 'Seoul: Enforced Exophony': 'I realised how it sounded for me, a Japanese person, to be harping on about the joys of venturing outside one's mother tongue—particularly here in Korea, where Japan had forced the Korean people into an exophonic condition against their will'.

As an Irish person, I'm writing this introduction in English because the British Empire lovingly forced its tongue on my great-grandparents. Across the late nineteenth and early twentieth century, my family—along with most of rural Ireland—dropped their native Gaeilge and transitioned to the language of colonial survival. I do speak Irish, but I largely taught myself; my parents only know a little.

In 'Weimar: Small Languages, Big Languages' Tawada describes the perceived pressure on writers to 'save' minority languages; it's particularly complicated when one isn't even a native speaker to begin with, and therefore risks—in the eyes of some—doing more harm than good. Still, most people want Irish to be spoken and written by as many as possible, if only to affirm that it's worth using at all. Colonial countries take it for granted that their language will be respected. For centuries ours was violently suppressed.

I used to think I would never write in Irish. Tawada has made me want to try. I defy you to come away from this book not yearning to explore something too—whether it's learning your first foreign language or simply reexamining the peculiarities of English.

Naoise Dolan
Dublin
April 2025

I
Voyages Outside the Mother Tongue

Dakar

Exophony as Common Sense

IN NOVEMBER OF 2002, I PARTICIPATED IN A SYM-
posium that took place in Dakar, Senegal. The symposium was
sponsored by the Goethe Institute, as well as the Center for Literary Research in Berlin, and a number of writers and scholars from
Germany, including myself, were invited to be in dialogue with a
group of Senegalese authors. It was there that I first heard the term
"exophonic writer," from a scholar named Robert Stockhammer. I
was familiar with similar terms, such as "immigrant literature" or
"creole literature," but "exophonic" had a much broader meaning,
referring to the general experience of existing outside of one's
mother tongue. It isn't just immigrants who write in foreign languages, after all, and it's not always the case that the languages
they write in are creole. The world is far more complex than that.

I was particularly struck by that complexity when I met the
German-language writers who had been invited to Senegal. For
example, both the Greek writer Eleni Torossi and I immigrated
to Germany, and I suppose to a certain extent you could call us
"immigrant writers." But someone like Maja Haderlap, a Slovenian writer who was born and raised in Austria, is decidedly
not an immigrant. Though she was raised in Austria, Haderlap
primarily grew up hearing and speaking Slovenian. Nowadays
in Austria this would be quite uncommon—but forty years ago,
there were still plenty of isolated pockets throughout the country
where minority languages were still spoken. While her parents
could speak German, Maja, who spent most of her time with her

3

Slovenian-speaking grandmother, didn't have a mother tongue, she said, so much as a grandmother tongue.

At the same symposium, the Swiss writer Hugo Loetscher spoke about language policies in Switzerland, which has four official languages. He explained the considerable differences that exist between spoken Swiss German and standard German, and what those differences mean for Swiss literature. It dawned on me that the phenomenon of existing outside of one's mother tongue was in fact quite common, and not necessarily related to being an immigrant or speaking a creole language.

In the former French colony of Senegal, it was the norm until recently for most books to be written in French—which meant that Senegalese writers were writing in a language other than the one they grew up hearing and speaking. Of course, oral literature had always been passed down in the local languages, but as written literature took on greater importance, writing in French was seen as the only choice. The kind of French that Senegalese writers were writing in was not a creole language, nor was it pidgin. When I asked whether there were any particular characteristics of Senegalese French, a young scholar from Berlin named Dirk Naguschewski informed me that my question was a fraught one. Most Senegalese writers dislike being associated with a "West African" style of French, as they see themselves as writing in standard French. I was surprised by his response—I had no idea that the pressure to adhere to standard French was so strong. I had assumed that, precisely because these highly educated writers were living in a pluralistic culture, it would be natural for a new kind of French—one distinct from the kind spoken in Paris—to develop there.

In Senegal, going to school and learning how to read and write meant learning how to read and write French, since for much of its history Wolof and other Indigenous Senegalese languages did not exist in written form. Whenever I admitted to someone in Senegal that I did not speak French, they seemed utterly perplexed. Perhaps they had never heard of a writer who didn't know French—after all, not knowing French basically amounted to saying that one was illiterate.

And yet, Senegalese writers have recently begun to publish books in Wolof. According to reports by publishers and editors, books written in Wolof have sold quite well, to the point that readership has increased overall—contrary to their expectations that these books would be difficult to sell.

Some Senegalese writers have also begun writing novels in English, such as Gorgui Dieng, who gave a presentation at the conference on his novel, *A Leap Out of the Dark*. While it might be a commonly held notion, at least in Japan, that the international language is English, in Senegal, it is French. English is considered just another European language.

When I left Dakar and traveled to Saint-Louis, another Senegalese city, I had to rely on my French-speaking German friends whenever I interacted with hotel staff or taxi drivers. All this is to say that, for a Senegalese writer, there is really no reason to write in English. Nevertheless I found it refreshing to learn that, when rebelling against a past in which they were forced to write in French, some Senegalese writers had opted not to return to their mother tongue of Wolof, but chose an altogether different language to write in, thereby broadening their own sense of autonomy and freedom. These writers were choosing to assert their independence not by reaching for the past and their roots, but by taking a leap into a completely different, faraway world.

Of course, the decision to write in English cannot be separated from the fact that a writer will almost certainly increase their global readership by doing so. In that sense, it may be difficult to argue that a writer is exactly exercising their own freedom of choice when they decide to write in English. Currently, there is a vigorous debate going on in Senegal over the politics of writing in English, as many writers confront the question of whether that is necessary in order to be read by more people all over the world.

Coming back to the term "exophony," however, I can't help but feel a fondness for the term, resonating as it does with the word "symphony." There are so many different kinds of music in the world. What happens when you step outside the cocoon of your own mother tongue? What new kinds of music do you begin to hear? Though "exophonic" might seem similar to concepts like "immigrant" or "foreign," I think it's exactly the opposite. The terms "immigrant literature" and "foreign literature" conjure images of an outsider coming in and taking up the domestic language in order to write something. "Exophonic literature," on the other hand, implies that a writer is going from the inside out. How do I step outside of the mother tongue to which I am bound? What might happen if I did? The exophonic is an adventurous concept, brimming with curiosity. Not all instances of exophonic literature are born out of such inquisitiveness, of course. Sometimes a writer is made to write in a language that is not their own due to colonization or exile. And yet, if the literature produced by such circumstances is beautiful and interesting, I see no need to place it in a separate category from other kinds of exophonic writing. At least, this is the conclusion I have come to after talking with a number of refugee writers in Germany over the past ten years. Many of them have told me that, while the circumstances of having to leave their country were of course painful, the encounter with a new language was not necessarily so.

The same could be said of formerly colonized countries. This is not at all to justify colonization; rather, we have to take seriously the work of those who are writing with the material they have been given, even if that material is less than ideal. According to

Dr. Stockhammer, all creative language is chosen. Writers from formerly colonized countries, who were forced to write in another language due to circumstances beyond their control, would then cease to be the exception. After all, even monolingual writers must write in a chosen language—otherwise, we would not be able to call what they write "literature." The phenomenon of exophony thus turns the tables on writers of so-called normal literature, by posing the question: Why did *you* choose to write in this particular language?

Many fierce debates took place at the Dakar conference. There was one scholar of French literature who had been living in Dakar for the past thirty years. She was a passionate supporter of Senegalese writers—but her attitude toward them bordered on the paternalistic. At one point, she made a well-intentioned but problematic comment along the lines of: "When you write in French, you must be very careful not to let your language get too rough around the edges. Otherwise, people will label your writing as 'African French' [here she used a racist word], and it won't be taken seriously." Even though I was listening to her commentary through an interpreter, I could hear the infantilization seeping out through the edges of her words. During the Q and A, Dirk Naguschewski pushed back on her comment, asserting that Senegalese writers were allowed to write however they wanted, and that just because this scholar happened to be a "native speaker" of French did not give her the license to determine what was good or bad French.

In Germany, I sometimes meet people who think they have absolute ownership over the German language simply because they are native speakers. They believe that the German in which Goethe wrote represents the pinnacle of the language, that the German in which Kleist wrote is slightly inferior to Goethe's, and that the German in which immigrants write is slightly inferior to Kleist's. I suppose people who haven't thought too deeply about literature might pick out a word in a text by an immigrant writer and deem it childish. Or they might see a sentence construction they aren't familiar with and assume it is bad writing. This sort of thing is not uncommon. If the critic and the writer share a mother tongue, the critic will tend to restrain their criticism; whereas if the writer is a "foreigner," they feel no qualms about broadcasting their ignorant opinions. Sometimes critics feel insecure about their grasp of contemporary literature and choose to project their inferiority complex onto immigrant writers. Perhaps in these cases, they see immigrant writing as something they feel entitled to police, to make sure it doesn't veer off in the "wrong direction."

In Japan, immigrant writing isn't a frequent topic of debate, as it's not enough of a major genre yet. Of course, there are many writers of Chinese or Korean heritage, but they still fall within the mainstream of Japanese-language literature, and would not necessarily be considered "minority" writers. The only writers that come to mind who have immigrated to Japan and write in Japanese as non-native speakers are Hideo Levy and David Zoppetti. Up until recently, many Japanese people believed it was impossible for someone whose mother tongue was not Japanese to write literature in their language. Levy has written about this phenomenon extensively in his essays.

If a writer decides to write in a particular language, they are under no obligation to use that language in the same way that the majority of its speakers use it. The writer is also not obligated to share the aesthetic sensibilities of their contemporaries. What's more important is that they uncover some latent potential in the language, which no one had noticed before. Venturing outside of one's mother tongue is one strategy for revealing the possibility or impossibility of a given linguistic expression. Of course, there are many ways to "step outside" of oneself, and taking up a foreign language is just one.

The most difficult aspect of writing in a foreign language is not the words themselves, but the constant need to battle against stereotypes. Many people—in both Germany and Japan—insist on measuring one's relationship to a foreign language using only the metrics of good or bad, skilled or unskilled. Turning to someone who has just uttered an incredibly complex aesthetic statement in Japanese, and saying, "Wow, your Japanese is so good" is like turning to Van Gogh and saying, "Wow, you're so good with sunflowers." But unfortunately, many people still make comments like these in complete earnest. For some reason, if the writer is a foreigner, it seems the only criterion for judging their relationship to the language they write in is "good" or "bad."

I think Japanese people often take up the study of a foreign language without thinking too deeply about their reasons for doing so. There, too, "good" and "bad" become the only way of defining their relationship to the language. There is probably a historical reason for this. In Japanese society, European languages (especially English and French) have long been used as a tool to enforce classist ideas. It's not just that being "bad" at English has implications for one's future, such as failing the entrance exams and not being able to go to college. There is a way that knowledge of a foreign language is used performatively, to reinforce one's status. Recently I was reading a Japanese manga and came across the sentence: "This is a French restaurant, so naturally everything on the menu is in French. For high-class customers only!" Learning a foreign language, and spending time abroad, are associated with becoming "high class"—in other words, putting distance between yourself and other, presumably more "ordinary," Japanese people. It becomes a status symbol, which implies that the authority for determining whether one is "good" or "bad" at a language comes not from within oneself, but from somewhere else. And for Japanese people, that place is occupied by the abstract image of a

"Westerner": It is his authority that determines whether they are "good" or "bad." This isn't just rooted in Confucianism—it's also a colonial idea. In a master-disciple relationship, a teacher is an actual, flesh-and-blood human being—not an abstract idol. However, to revere the abstract image of the "Westerner" as an agent of authority means, simultaneously, to deny the individuality of actual people in Europe and the United States. Actual, living, flesh-and-blood "Westerners" are quite diverse. They are Turkish German, Korean German, Indian British, Vietnamese French, African American, Japanese American, etc. But the concept of the "Westerner" allows Japanese people to completely ignore this diversity and instead cling to an abstract image they have in their head. At least, this was the case in until recently.

Back when I was still living in Japan almost twenty years ago, I saw a film at the Athénée Français called "The Dog That Was Hit by a Car." The film told the story of a West African scholar who lived in Japan. One day, he is approached by a group of French expats in a bar who ask him why he is studying Japanese culture when there are people starving in Africa. "Is it true that they eat human flesh in Africa?" a drunk man asks. In a flash of anger, the scholar flips over the table. Previously in the film, he had decided to teach French to make money on the side, and had posted flyers advertising his classes. Most of the interested students were young Japanese women, but when they arrived at his house and discovered that he was African, they were frightened and ran away. This scene throws into sharp relief the warped desires that Japanese people have vis-à-vis the French language, as well as the feeling of unease that stems from their own sense of inferiority. Perhaps subconsciously, the women in the film are thinking, "Even though we Asians were once considered barbarians by the European just like Africans, now that we are rich, we can pay the expensive fees required to learn French, thus proving that we are no longer barbarians." And yet, when an African man turns out to be the French teacher, they run away in shock. All of this means that, somewhere along the way, Japanese people have inherited the racism of Europeans. This strange inferiority complex may have been concealed for a time by Japan's rapid economic growth, but it never really disappeared. I was born at a time when Japanese people were still trying to heal the wounds of war, asserting that they were "on par" with the West by flaunting their money.

When I first immigrated to Germany in 1980, I noticed that it was always older Japanese people who would say things like: "Nowadays, we're the ones dining at the best restaurants in Europe and taking home the most expensive things." Perhaps this was their way of dealing with the stress that came from having to constantly conceal their own sense of inferiority. It would be one thing to indulge yourself at the height of the bubble economy, but I sensed something else—a certain aggressiveness to their frenzied shopping sprees, a desperation to rid themselves of their self-hatred by spending money. As a result, not only did we lose the opportunity to really analyze our Eurocentrism and destroy it—we also equated European culture with consumerism, and came to identify with it. And we that, we swept the eraser shavings of history off the table and into the trash.

Recently, I heard a Japanese person say they were "going to Asia." At first I had no idea what they were talking about, but eventually I realized that they didn't think of Japan as part of Asia. To them, "Asia" was not a geographical entity, so much as an economic zone.

Some people accuse me of being anachronistic when I talk about the inferiority complex of Japanese people, implying that it's no longer relevant. *I'm just learning French because it's fun*, they claim. *There are so many things I want to buy in Paris and French food is so delicious! I don't have an inferiority complex, I'm not resentful, there's no need to think about anything difficult or complicated!* But the intertwined problems of Eurocentrism and Japan's deeply twisted sense of nationalism have yet to be overcome—they have simply been concealed. If only the economic crisis had led to a real reckoning with these issues, perhaps the collapse of the bubble economy wouldn't have been for nothing. But of course, it was never that simple. As soon as the bubble economy collapsed and the era of luxury ended, the needle simply shifted: The new line became about how studying a foreign language like French was an unnecessary indulgence, and how one should study a more practical and business-oriented language like English. Meanwhile Japanese universities continue slashing the budgets of every language program except for English.

If you don't think too deeply or seriously about why you are studying a language, you end up becoming a pawn of your country's opportunism.

These are just some of the things I was thinking about on the plane ride back from Senegal, as I munched on the delicious snacks provided by Air France.

Berlin
The Spell of Colonialism

IN JANUARY OF 2002, THERE WAS AN ACADEMIC CON-
ference in Berlin on the late Romantic writer Heinrich von
Kleist—one of my favorite nineteenth-century writers. A young
Hungarian scholar of German literature proposed a panel for the
last day with scholars from France, Hungary, and Japan. If you're
wondering why these three countries in particular, it's because
those are the only places where Kleist's collected works have been
published. There has never been a *Collected Works of Heinrich von
Kleist* in English.

The organizers of the conference didn't have enough money
to invite a "real" Kleist scholar from Japan, so they invited me
instead—not as a specialist, but as a local amateur (in the literal
sense, meaning "lover"). I was asked to give a short presentation
on the *Collected Works of Kleist* and describe the history of its
Japanese translations. So I took that opportunity to read not only
the most current one, but also the first: Mori Ogai's translation
of Kleist's "The Betrothal in St. Domingo" (though Ogai titled
this "Evil Destiny" in Japanese) as well as "Earthquake in Chile."

Reading about foreign language education and the status of
translation in Japan around the dawn of the twentieth century, I
realized that there was a big difference between the circumstances
under which Ogai and I had studied German. After the Meiji
Restoration, Japan invited foreign professors to come and teach
at Japanese universities as part of its mission to adopt European
languages, technology, and sciences. At the time there were very

few Japanese textbooks on science or even Japanese professors who could teach at the university level: All classes at the University of Tokyo medical school were then taught in German. So the relationship that university students had to foreign languages at that time was very different than it is now. They had no choice but to learn them: Other languages would be part of their future whether they liked it or not. I respect their dedication, but I'm also grateful to have been born at a time when "the West" wasn't assumed to be the ultimate authority on things, and when it wasn't unusual for a girl to go abroad and study German. The public high school I went to in Japan used to be an it was an all-boys school, and German was the primary foreign language taught. After World War II, it became coed, but German courses were still offered. My first encounter with German was at that school. In college, I majored in Russian literature, but continued studying German at the Waseda language institute.

I imagine Mori Ogai must have had mixed feelings about the changes taking place around him. He went to Germany and chose to study the new science of "hygiene" at a time when Japan was hurtling down a road to modernity predicted on a strong military—modeled on Prussia—and bent on greater wealth. At the same time, Ogai always maintained a certain degree of skepticism toward the discourse of "civilization and enlightenment"—in other words, Westernization. How many Japanese exchange students or military personnel from that time would have shared his view? In Berlin, Ogai distanced himself from other Japanese people, choosing instead to live on Luisenstrasse (now the site of the Mori Ogai Memorial Museum). This distancing suggests to me that his opinions may not always have meshed with those of other Japanese students in Berlin.

In Ogai's story "A Great Discovery," the protagonist, who has just arrived in Berlin from Japan, goes to pay his respects to a

Japanese diplomat. The diplomat makes fun of him for being unfamiliar with the big city and calls him a country bumpkin. For him, the West is to Japan what the city is to the country. The diplomat asks the protagonist what he came here to do, and the protagonist replies that he is here because he's been instructed to learn about hygiene. To which the diplomat replies, "Hygiene!? You're joking, right? What good is hygiene going to do for a people who still walk around wearing straw sandals and picking their noses in public?" Did Europeans, the protagonist wonders, really never pick their noses? He can't get the question out of his head the entire time he is in Germany. He wonders whether it isn't more unhygienic to blow your nose into a handkerchief, pick your nose with it, and then put that same handkerchief back into your pocket. I think Ogai was trying to describe something we would now call "cultural relativism," which would have been totally incompatible with the framework of civilizational hierarchy prevalent at the time.

At the end of the story, the protagonist is reading a European novel and comes across a description of a character picking his nose. He feels vindicated, ecstatic. The humor of the story lies in the fact that the protagonist's "discovery" is not a glamorous scientific one, but the simple fact that Europeans also pick their noses. Yet the work is also important because it critiques the myth of "hygiene" altogether. After all, for Europeans, cleanliness was godliness and this "cleanliness" was used as a yardstick to measure how "civilized" a country was. In this way, "hygiene" was used to enforce racism. There is of course the Nazi pseudoscience of "eugenics" and "phrenology," but "hygiene" is no less dangerous a concept.

Eventually Japanese people stopped walking around in straw sandals (*zori* and *waraji*) and started wearing Western shoes. A lot of people today assume that this happened automatically. They view history as a natural phenomenon rather than something that human beings make themselves, and are responsible for making. As though if you left a pair of zori out long enough, they would naturally morph into shoes, the same way tadpoles transform into frogs. But reading Ogai shows you that it wasn't like that. Japan forced its own citizens to start wearing Western shoes. After all, this was a time when the West was all-powerful, and there was still a real possibility that Japan might be colonized. If Japanese people had continued wearing zori, the West might have continued to view Japan as an "uncivilized" country, and unequal treaties may have kept it in a semicolonized state. Obviously Japan didn't want that, so things like coed bathing, nudism, homosexuality, and other behaviors that the United States considered "uncivilized" were banned and even criminalized, effectively disappearing from society altogether. It's not that they went away on their own, but that people made them go away. However, this wasn't entirely the Americans' fault. The problem was more that this type of thinking—captured so well by the diplomat character in Ogai's story—became dominant in the minds of Japanese people themselves. Ogai's brief description of the diplomat's attitude conveys much more than a textbook or even a historical novel ever could. It gives us something like the texture of history itself.

By the time I was in elementary school in the 1960s, the Meiji Restoration was already a thing of the past. But after reading Ogai, I realized that even as late as the sixties, "hygiene" was still part of many educational programs in Japan. I had to bring a handkerchief or a pack of tissues to school every day; teachers inspected us to see whether our nails were properly clipped; they made us sing a song about washing our hands with soap and water. All of this was a byproduct of a time when Japan was desperately trying to Westernize and become a first-world country. I wish I could say that I had rebelled and refused to wash my hands, but the fact that I obediently followed the rules and washed my hands makes me feel like a real child of the colonies. Once at a party in Senegal I overheard some Europeans complaining that they had to remind the woman who cooked for them to wash her hands every day, otherwise she wouldn't do it. I am certain that similar conversations must have happened between white people who lived in Japan around the time of the Meiji Restoration.

For the most part, I think people should mind their own business and worry about their own hygiene rather than other people's. But most Japanese people seem to assume that if something is "Western," it must be correct (there are exceptions of course, such as Tanizaki's *In Praise of Shadows*). Their attitude toward hygiene, which borders on the obsessive, is a perfect example of this. To this day, you will not find another country that has roads and airports and floors as clean as Japan's. It's even gotten to the point that people make themselves sick because they are too clean. Once, I heard a German person say on TV that they imagined Japanese people must think Germans are dirty compared to them. So the tables have simply been turned. Maybe hearing a European say this might heal Japan's inferiority complex temporarily, but ultimately the Japanese are still victims of the hygiene myth. It's like a woman battling misogyny and prejudice as she fights her way up the corporate ladder, only to be told she is too "mannish." Most likely this will not make her happy at all. On the contrary, she may suffer from exhaustion and self-loathing, and even become depressed. It might even happen that all the stress she's accumulated over time suddenly explodes—and she becomes an ultranationalist.

In any case, Ogai's text, a blend of essay and short story, conveys the feeling of history better than any historical novel ever could, casting a critical eye on the concept of hygiene at a moment when Japan was unquestioningly adopting it. In comparison, his translation of Kleist leaves something to be desired. Although it's impressive that Ogai introduced this author to Japan so early on, he prunes and overly shapes Kleist's prose. This is a shame, because Kleist's style broke up the classical balance of German prose and cleared the way for new possibilities in the language. He often uses complex sentences with numerous dependent clauses, but those clauses don't just give the reader more information—instead they seem to have a life of their own, sprouting up one after another. His style is an essential part of his charm, inseparable from the content of his texts.

For example, the first sentence of his story "The Duel" seems at first to describe a family tree. But as more and more dependent clauses keep piling on, we learn about a child who was born out of wedlock, and of another child who was born as a result of an affair but soon died, and also about a duke who grows estranged from his half brother because of the latter's affair, to the point that it's unclear who is going to inherit the family fortune. In this way Kleist unfurls a complex family tree with multiple branches.

The first sentence of "The Marquise of O" is extremely long as well. In the same breath as it introduces a well-to-do lady who is married and pregnant, it reveals that she has placed an ad in the newspaper searching for the father of her child, and the fact that all of this is conveyed in one extended sentence makes it feel as though Kleist's language is opening up a giant hole in the supposedly unshakable bourgeois family system. If that long sentence had been cut up into shorter ones, it would have changed the meaning entirely: it would imply that although A (the marriage system) exists, B (an unusual incident) happened—and that's not at all what Kleist is saying. The length of the sentence is itself meaningful.

The first sentence of "Earthquake in Chile" is also extremely long, and while at first it posits itself as a mere chronology, because the earthquake and the execution are packed together in the same sentence, the reader feels almost dizzy from the way this sense of simultaneity is lodged into history. But in Ogai's translation, these features of Kleist's style are lopped off like so many extraneous branches that might spoil an otherwise beautiful view, and I find that very regrettable.

Ogai wasn't the only one who took this approach to Kleist's style, though. To this day I hear academics, critics, and translators from every country bemoaning his "terrible writing." When I hear that, I get so angry it makes the blood rush to my head, which then makes me want to cool off by jumping into the Kleine Wannsee in Berlin, where Kleist and Henriette Vogel killed themselves.

There is no objectively correct length for a sentence. The length of a sentence is one of its modes of expression. When I read Kleist's sentences, I feel a deep sense of joy that comes from the language permeating my brain. Any style that can absorb the trembling that arises from this joy and cause an earthquake that unsettles the landscape of history cannot be labeled "terrible writing." But the fact that I can even get on my high horse and make these critiques is only possible because in the last hundred years, many different theories of translation have been introduced, and I'm fortunate enough to have been exposed to them.

Of course, our expectations about literature have also changed quite a bit since the Meiji and Taisho periods, when it was more common to think of a writer as the representative of a particular nation state. When the Japanese literary magazine *Bungei* published a special issue on Kleist in 1911, there were quite a few critics who praised him for being an exemplary Prussian writer.

These days, it would be pretty rare to find someone who is studying German because they admire Prussia. It's more likely they would be thinking about what aspects of Prussia failed, and what aspects of Japan, which tried to model itself after Prussia, failed as well. All the more reason to read Kleist's prose, then, which attempts to escape the idea of Prussia altogether, and even demolish it.

Los Angeles
The Poetic Ravine Between Languages

IN 1997, I SPENT A COUPLE OF MONTHS IN VILLA AU-
rora, near Santa Monica, California. This beautiful Mexican-style
villa once belonged to Lion Feuchtwanger, a Jewish refugee who
lived there after fleeing the Nazis. These days, the villa functions
as a residency for artists, filmmakers, authors, and composers
based in Germany. Thomas Mann's former house is just around the
corner. Bertolt Brecht, whose photo adorns the villa's living room
wall, lived there, and Schoenberg came there often. It wasn't just
German novelists and musicians who spent time there. Adorno
and Horkheimer, members of the Frankfurt School, lived in Los
Angeles for a while as well.

Fleeing fascist Germany to seek asylum in the United States
during World War II is not so different from fleeing dictatorships in
Eastern Europe or the Middle East to seek asylum in Germany. The
main difference is that almost all refugees these days take up writing
in German. In contrast, Jewish refugees who fled Germany during
the war continued to write in German even when they lived in the
United States, and some even returned to Germany after the war.

I was vaguely aware that Thomas Mann had lived in exile in the
United States, but I'd never come across any references to California in his writing, nor was I aware of him ever writing anything
in English. I can recall various places that have appeared in his
work, such as Lübeck or Hamburg, or the Engadin in Switzerland, or even Venice, but I have no memory of ever encountering
the distinctive landscape of California anywhere in his writing.

Later I went and checked his collected works and actually found a short essay that he'd written in English. But it wasn't a literary work. It was more of a public letter to America, written with some stylistic flair.

In an obituary for Stefan Heym that Matthias Wegner wrote in the *Neue Zürcher Zeitung*, he observes: "Most German writers have not been especially international in their outlook or even bilingual. At the very least, that was true of more generations than not. There were a handful of exceptions, especially among those who were forced into exile by the Nazis. Even then, however, very few writers were willing or able to change the language in which they wrote. Klaus Mann and Erich Maria Remarque stand out for their ability to wield total control over more than one language. And then there was Stefan Heym, who wrote many novels in English. In fact, he continued writing in English even after he returned to Germany."

The reason that German-language authors are not exophonically inclined is not lack of linguistic talent. Even contemporary German authors whose English is very good, and who have lived in the English-speaking world for many years, rarely write in English. Take Anne Duden, who has lived in London for over twenty years, or W. G. Sebald or Ulrike Draesner, who lived in England. None of these writers ever wrote in English, despite having excellent command of the language. Sebald, who lived in England for over twenty-five years, was once asked by an audience member why he didn't write in English. He replied that he'd written plenty of academic papers in English, but that literature was completely different. At the time, I understood what he was saying, at least on an intuitive level. But over the past decade or so, I've written many books that have chipped away at that idea, and now I don't think I agree with it at all.

Anne Duden gave a more concrete answer to a similar question.

She said that the German language contains the history of the German people, and to distance herself from it would mean being unable to access that history. This is why she couldn't bring herself to stop writing in German. By that I don't think she meant that she was proud of German history, but that she felt responsible for it.

In Duden's lectures on poetry at Paderborn University, she juxtaposes the words *schrei* (scream) and *schreiben* (to write). At a sonic and a semantic level, these two words have a complex relationship. But people who can turn their screams into language tend to live in somewhat privileged circumstances. To be able to choose the kind of education you want, to have the luxury of writing poems and novels, is quite rare. Most people are not given a voice at all. Instead they die with silent screams on their lips, their eyes flung wide open as they watch the destruction around them. To write is not the same thing as to scream. And yet, if writing were cut off from the act of screaming, it would no longer be literature. The act of screaming is inseparable from the act of writing. Though the two words do not share an etymology, they are intimately bound together through a person's lived experiences.

There are other aspects of the German language that are important architecturally to Duden's writing. In German, the meaning of a verb can change depending on the prefix. So even if two words appear to be opposite in meaning, they are often connected at a deeper level. In fact, you can use a hyphen to combine them into one word, without repeating the main verb. For example, in Duden's lectures on poetry, she uses the phrase *Unter-und-Auftauchen*. In this case, the first word, *untertauchen*, means "to hide, submerge," while *auftauchen* means "to emerge, appear, surface." But these two words are not simple antonyms. For Duden, they are inextricable: When someone stands in front of a painting, the subject submerges themselves in the image, and language emerges through that process.

Technically you can't combine verbs this way in Japanese, but if you could, it might look something like this. Take the words *taizai*, which means a stay or sojourn, and *sonzai*, which means existence. The second character of each of these words, *zai*, is the same, so in order to highlight the continuities between "sojourning" and "existing" I might write *tai/son • zai*:

滞 / 存・在

When I think about writers who lived in California, I also think of the poet Hiromi Ito. In 2002, I saw an English-language performance of hers in Innsbruck. I still vividly remember the feeling of a different language invading my body. My cells screamed in refusal, yet seemed to devour the words at the same time, expanding and becoming pregnant with them. I felt the sunshine of California in her voice. But it didn't conjure cheerfulness and health so much as a kind of static electricity that induced defiance and response.

Why wasn't Thomas Mann more like Hiromi Ito? It seems like a simple question but it's actually quite complex. Because Mann's work is not filled with California sunshine, you might assume that he hated the place, burying himself in the dark closet of the German language as he continued writing his books. But Mann was apparently charmed by the pleasant climate and landscape of California. Back then, California didn't yet have the reputation of a warm, comfortable place that it has now. If anything, the majority of German authors living in exile there struggled to adapt to the climate. Leonhard Frank once said that in California "there is no air inside the air." He complained about the lack of seasons, describing Hollywood as a hell "where one is permanently exposed to the sun, far removed from life." As a result of his antiwar activities in World War I, Frank ended up becoming stateless in 1934, at the age of fifty-two. He lived in exile in New York, eventually relocating to Los Angeles, but in the end he couldn't adapt and went back to New York. He didn't return to Germany until 1950, at the age of sixty-eight. Similarly, Carl Zuckmayer once went so far as to say that "in California, nature is lifeless and eerie. When I look upon the garish-colored roses blooming in the yard at Christmas, it makes me want to vomit." Brecht, too, never managed to acclimate. He once said that "just glancing out the window here fills me with grief." This, of course, had less to do with California's climate and more to do with Hollywood being a symbol of commercialism, where even the sun sports a dazzling smile.

As I looked out the window of Lion Feuchtwanger's study each day and saw the ocean, I was struck by the thought that this was the same Pacific Ocean that had filled my heart with such longing as a child—only now I was looking at it from the other side. But I had no desire to return to Tokyo. People generally feel nostalgia for their homeland when they can't accept, acknowledge, or understand the culture of the place they are living in. But I felt that there were plenty of people in Japan who didn't understand me, and plenty of people in California who did. It has always seemed to me that cultural differences are relative. I never felt the need to idealize the place where I was from.

What I felt when I looked at the Pacific Ocean wasn't nostalgia. In fact, it was something like the opposite. After leaving Tokyo and crossing Siberia to reach Europe, then crossing the Atlantic Ocean to come to America, then crossing the North American continent and finally ending up in California, the so-called end of the world, I had the strange feeling that I had actually come full circle and ended up right where I started. I could viscerally sense the roundness of the earth.

In the past, people who move frequently might have been pitied as wanderers who didn't belong anywhere. But nowadays, constant movement has become the norm. It's not that such people belong nowhere—rather, they have heavy eyelids that allow them to sleep deeply wherever they go, tongues that can understand multiple languages, and compound eyes that can focus wherever they are. Isn't this more important? Nothing good can come from a predetermined sense of community. I want to believe that living means creating new communities wherever we happen to be, using the power of language.

Los Angeles was hot, especially downtown, but Feuchtwanger's house, built on a hill in the Pacific Palisades, was cool and comfortable. The day I arrived, I opened my window and didn't close it again for the entire two months that I was there. It never rained, and no draft blew in at night. It was never too cold or too hot. Coming from Hamburg, the weather in California felt like a gift, and I was incredibly grateful for it. After a while, though, I started to feel bored by the eternally cloudless sky. I wasn't making progress on my manuscript. In northern Germany, where I usually live, winter is when I am most productive, as it is the time of year with the fewest hours of sunlight. As I ignore the darkness beyond the window, face my manuscript, and begin to write, light begins to flood my brain, as though it is its own electricity source. Writing brings more sunshine than going for a walk. Which is why I make so much progress when it's dark out.

Earlier I said that German writers don't tend to write in languages other than German, but this isn't the case for Austrian and Swiss people. Sabine Scholl, an Austrian writer who used to live in the United States, once told me that she made a concerted effort to write in English. Since there is already a gap between High German and Austrian German, I suspect many Austrians also view the idea of a "mother tongue" with some skepticism. There are many examples of French writers writing in languages other than French, though they regard their own language highly. Adelbert von Chamisso wrote in German, and Eastern European writers have always written in many languages.

Of course, it's not as though English never appears in the work of German writers, even those who write exclusively in German. Sometimes it comes up in the work of Anne Duden in the form of a quote or reference, or as a distant voice. The same can be said of Patrick Roth, who lived in Los Angeles for over twenty-five years. Once, I went to his house and was struck by the way he arranged his books. I couldn't figure out the logic behind it. They weren't arranged in alphabetical order, by nationality, time period, or theme. When I finally asked him, he said that all of his books had fallen on the floor one time after a big earthquake, and he'd simply put them back on the shelves haphazardly. They had remained that way ever since. There was a certain appeal to this random system born from chaos. It occurred to me that the German writers who fled to California to escape the Nazis were like this too—books that had lost their place during a disaster had been randomly put back on the shelf wherever there was room.

Patrick Roth, however, came to the United States by choice, initially as an exchange student. In *Meine Reise zu Chaplin* (My journey to Chaplin) and other books he's written, it's clear he is deeply interested in film. When he speaks, he sounds no different than any other Californian, but he continues to write, determinedly, in German.

In other words, writing only in German doesn't necessarily mean that a German writer has no interest in other cultures. And yet, I can't help but feel that there is a certain limitation to writing in only one language. What is behind that choice?

When I give a reading in Germany, I'm sometimes asked, usually by a young person, whether I write as a German or a Japanese person. This question always perplexes me. I suppose I don't really understand the phrase "as a person of X country." I think inside of every person there is a mixture of many cultures and languages.

Young people in the United States are different from young

people in Europe. As expected in a country of immigrants, they feel complete ownership over their adopted country and language. Which is why Americans have never asked me whether I consider myself German or Japanese. Instead they ask why I don't write in English, since I am in America. I tell them that that would be quite difficult, and that writing in English is not something I'd be able to do right away, but they don't seem to understand. I consider myself quite open to adopting elements of other cultures, but it doesn't work that way with language. It takes a lot of effort to be able to speak a new language, let alone write in it. In order to internalize a language to the point where you can write a novel, it's not enough to store new vocabulary words away like crates in a warehouse—you have to continuously connect them to the ones you already know. And those connections aren't just made on a one-to-one basis either. Sometimes the introduction of one new word to your vocabulary can rearrange your entire organism, which consumes an enormous amount of energy.

Besides, I'm not interested in studying lots of languages. To me, it's the space between languages that's most important, more than the languages themselves. Maybe what I really want is not to be a writer of this or that language in particular, but to fall into the poetic ravine between them.

Paris
This Language Which Is Not One

IN JANUARY OF 2003, AS PART OF MY PRIZE PACKAGE
for winning the Bunkamura Deux Magots literary prize, I was
offered a trip to Paris to attend the award ceremony.

Around eleven o'clock in the morning, the café Deux Magots grew quiet as the last customers went home after breakfast.
Shortly afterward, the critics began to gather, clinking their
champagne glasses and puffing on their cigarettes as they began
their discussion. At last, one of them took the microphone and
announced: "This year's winner is Michka Assayas!" The crowd
erupted in applause, and a phone call went out to the winner.
We must have waited around thirty minutes or so before Assayas
arrived by car and entered the café, flooded by lights and camera
flashes. Although the names of the four authors short-listed for
the prize were listed on the letter of invitation, the winner was
only announced on the day of the ceremony. The prize committee
members seemed to reach their decision without much debate—
perhaps it had been unanimous. The café wasn't very large, and
was packed to the brim with people, some of whom were wedged
between tables. Once every few minutes a champagne glass would
fall and break. The air was filled with smoke and the murmuring
of voices. It was a peculiar, exciting atmosphere. If it had been
Japan or Germany, I wouldn't have been able to relax, as I would
have felt too much responsibility. But since I was in Paris, far from
home, I could simply relax and enjoy the event.

Afterward, I got off at the Odéon Metro station and wandered around for a bit. There was a shocking amount of bookstores. When I told Bernard Banoun, my French translator, that we didn't have this many bookstores in Germany, he said it only seemed that way because French culture is so concentrated in Paris. Besides, he continued, Germany has great bookstores all over the country, publishes more books, and has more readers than France overall. Not to mention there is much more financial and institutional support for writers, which makes it easier to make a living there than in France.

Later that night, I had dinner with Banoun and some other people from Éditions Verdier, my French publisher. Compared to the publishers I'd met in other countries, they seemed more immersed in their own literary world. Sometimes you hear people say that globalization has made the world more homogeneous, but that night convinced me otherwise. The Verdier people took me to an unpretentious-looking restaurant. Every aspect of the evening—from the photos on the wall, to the restaurant owner's odd collection of objects, to the scent and flavor of the duck and white bean stew, to the water that came in a fancy glass container, to the clothes people were wearing, to the expressions on their faces, to the questions the editor asked me—would have been unimaginable in Hamburg. How was it that a mere one-hour plane ride could take me to such a different world, one with no connection to English at all?

Banoun translated my observations into French for the other guests, but not without difficulty. He hesitated at first, saying he thought it would sound strange if he were to translate what I had said verbatim, though of course he would do it. Something about his hesitation struck me as profound. I've always been less interested in crossing borders than in dwelling in them. And in that moment of hesitation, I could sense the presence of a border: something beyond language itself.

The world would be a terribly boring place if it were to be completely overtaken by English, that shallow business language that can be understood anywhere. My intention here isn't to denigrate English, any more than it is to commend French. It simply struck me that it is moments like these—when the strange specificity of a place is foregrounded in all its richness—that compel us to cross borders in the first place.

The conversation that night touched on a wide array of topics, from photography, painting, language, and film, to the persecution of the Jews, to revolution, and polytheism. Then, out of the blue, someone asked me why I lived in Hamburg rather than Paris. I laughed in spite of myself, remembering the first time I came to Paris for a reading sometime in the early nineties. During the Q and A, someone asked me a question I'd never been asked in any other country: Why did I write in German, rather than French? Of course, I'd been asked plenty of times why I chose to write in a foreign language rather than in my mother tongue. But when I was asked why I didn't write in French specifically, I had no idea how to answer. "They can't imagine someone choosing German over French," a German person said to me after the event, chuckling a little. Still, I felt there was a clear difference between the American who told me I should write in English and the French person who said I should write in French.

Paul Celan, the German-language poet I admire most, lived in Paris throughout his later years, but never wrote in any language other than German. Come to think of it, the second time I ever went to Paris was for an international conference on Celan. Afterward, a student took me to Celan's grave, in the suburbs of Paris. The bus took forever to come, and when it finally dropped us off at the graveyard, we were the only ones there. Hundreds of identical, square gravestones stretched on and on in neat rows. They lay flat on the ground, illuminated by the setting sun. For some reason, my heart began to beat more quickly. A man who looked like he might be a groundskeeper appeared, and when we asked him where Ancel's grave was, he told us right away. As most people know, "Celan" was the poet's pen name, an anagram of his actual name, Ancel. He was born to German-speaking Jewish parents from Czernowitz, which was under Romanian rule at the time. Celan once said that "a poet can only write poetry in one language." And indeed, he continued to write poetry in German—the same language spoken by the people who murdered his mother and friends—till the day he died.

Celan had an incredible gift for languages. Not only was his French excellent, he also translated Mandelstam's poems from Russian. In this sense, Celan was similar to Kafka: Both grew up speaking German as a minority language in a multilingual Eastern European context.

But when he talks about the poet only being able to write in "one language," I don't think he's talking about language in the usual sense. Celan's "German" also included French and Russian, and not simply as loanwords. Instead, the languages are twined together like a net that constitutes the foundation for his poetic expression. Which is why when Celan says "one language," it is more akin to what Walter Benjamin says about translation: It brings languages "face-to-face" with each other.

Take the first few lines of one of Celan's most well-known poems:

Bei Wein und Verlorenheit, bei
beider Neige:

ich ritt durch den Schnee, hörst du,
ich ritt Gott in die Ferne—die Nähe, er sang

With wine and lostness, with
both dwindling:

I rode through the snow, you hear?
I rode God into the far—the near, he sang

In the first line, you have the word *Neige* (lessening, dwindling), and then suddenly, in the next line, *Schnee* (snow) appears. Semantically, the words for "dwindling" and "snow" have nothing to do with each other. But the word *Neige* which means "dwindling" in German also means "snow" in French. In that sense, "dwindling" and "snow" are intimately connected. They don't share the same etymology or pronunciation, but visually they are identical. One only has to read Freud's *Interpretation of Dreams* to understand to what extent we are controlled by the "chance resemblance" between words.

For Celan, this resemblance is not sonic, but imagistic. People often say that the history of European poetry is primarily rooted in sound rather than text (with some rare exceptions like the Concrete Poetry movement). But Celan thinks graphically more than sonically. It is worth remembering that Celan's spouse was a graphic designer who left behind numerous etchings to be published alongside his poems.

To me, Celan's poems have a multilingual structure akin to a magic net that even captures Japanese, a language he never knew. I have written about this in my essay collection *Katakoto no Uwagoto* (Incoherent babblings), so I won't repeat myself here. Suffice it to say that the more I read Celan, the more I am convinced that what he refers to as "one language" is not one language at all. This is why I have no special preference for authors who write in multiple languages. Even if you never set foot outside your mother tongue, it is still possible to create multiple languages within it—so that concepts such as "inside" and "outside" become irrelevant altogether.

Cape Town

What Language Do You Dream In?

PEOPLE OFTEN ASK WHAT LANGUAGE I DREAM IN, A question I always find slightly annoying. Implicit in the question is the assumption that it's impossible for people to truly speak two languages—that one of them must be the "fake" language and the other must be the "real" language. There is a word in Japanese for this: *nimaijita*, or fork-tongued, which implies that those who speak two languages are liars. Here are some related questions I recall people asking me over the years: "I know Japanese is your mother tongue, but aren't you basically German at this point?" "No matter how long you speak German, won't your soul always be Japanese?" "Which language do you feel like you can express your true self in?" "Essentially," "soul," "true self"—I despise phrases like these. People seem to have a burning desire to know which language corresponds to the "real" me. They assume that however skilled I may be at crafting lies in my fake language while I'm awake, the real me only emerges in my dreams, in my "true" language.

But the truth is that the real me speaks multiple languages, so in my dreams I speak multiple languages too. I don't just dream in German and Japanese—I also have dreams where I'm struggling to speak English, or some other language like Polish that I don't recall ever having studied. I even have nightmares in Spanish sometimes, a language I don't speak a word of. In this particular nightmare, I'm standing in front of an audience, getting ready to read my work. When I look closely at my manuscript, however, it's written in Spanish, and I can't understand it at all, though the words on the page are undoubtedly my own. My heart begins to pound, cold sweat trickles down my forehead, I feel like I'm suffocating—and suddenly, I wake up. There is a saying in German: *Das kommt mir Spanisch vor* ("It's all Spanish to me"), meaning something is completely unintelligible. Perhaps that is where my nightmare comes from—after all, dreams are sometimes literal manifestations of idiomatic phrases. Which tells me that I am probably dreaming in German, since the story in my nightmare is a literalization of a German phrase.

In any case, I was so annoyed by the question about what language I dream in that it prompted me to write a novel, *Bioskop der Nacht* (Night bioscope), about a girl who dreams in a language she cannot understand. The language in her dream is slightly "off"—it sounds somewhat similar to German, but it's a language she's never heard before. Eventually she meets a Dutch person and learns that the language in her dream is Afrikaans, which was originally spoken by Dutch people who came to South Africa, then developed into its own language. To Dutch people from the Netherlands, Afrikaans apparently sounds like a slightly outdated version of Dutch. To me, however, it's always sounded quite interesting: I'm able to pick up some words here and there because of its proximity to German, but I can't quite make out what the person is saying—almost as if I were dreaming. For example, the word *lecker* in German means "delicious," and is only used to describe food; whereas in Dutch and Afrikaans, you can use it to describe anything from weather to clothing to people. So in Afrikaans, it often sounds to me as if people are saying, "The weather is quite delicious today, isn't it?" "These clothes are delicious!" or "That person is really delicious." The protagonist in my novel has never been to South Africa, nor does she have any friends or relatives from there. In other words, the language that she dreams in, which is allegedly supposed to express her "true" self, is a language spoken in a faraway country that has nothing to do with her at all. Not understanding why this is happening, she decides to go to Cape Town.

At this point in the story, I stopped writing, and decided I needed to go to South Africa myself to finish doing research for the book. It was the summer of 2000. By summer I mean, of course, that it was summer in Germany, but winter in South Africa. Even so, it turned out that winter in Cape Town was much warmer than summer in Hamburg.

The day I arrived, the Concorde crashed. But it wasn't the plane crash itself that shocked me so much as the fact that the same news was being broadcast on TV in eleven different languages simultaneously. The exact same images flashed across the screen on each channel, but the words describing them were completely different. I was struck by the sudden realization then that the media is poor in images, but rich in language. While images are universal, language insists on difference. Among the eleven languages being broadcast that day, I only recognized two: English and Afrikaans. The rest were Indigenous languages I had never heard before. For example, Xhosa: I knew that this language used a variety of click consonants, but when I actually heard it being spoken on TV, I didn't recognize it for what it was. This was my first trip to the African continent, and I wondered how it was possible for a country to maintain eleven official languages, as South Africa did. When I visited Senegal two years later, I found it to be nothing at all like South Africa. But in both places, it was language that initially drew me in and allowed me to have a relationship with it.

Africa is a place in which many languages once coexisted, until Europeans came along and colonized it, enforcing their own languages onto the people there. But when the colonial period ended and most Europeans went home, there was a dispute over which of the Indigenous languages would become the official language of each country. In cases like Senegal, most people agreed that they should keep French as the official language, since whatever language they chose would be unlikely to be spoken by the majority of Senegalese people. And then there were cases like South Africa, which decided to have eleven official languages. I was shocked that this could even be a possibility. Wouldn't such a lack of linguistic unity create social and educational problems? At the same time, I couldn't help but wonder what such multilingualism might make possible.

The phenomenon of multilingualism cannot simply be written off as a problem unique to "developing" countries—although many people in industrialized countries will point to the multilingualism of Africa as proof of an "underdeveloped" civilization. In Germany, for example, some people argue that they had already created a standard, written language a long time ago, back when Martin Luther translated the Bible into German. And now that we live in an age in which English—the language of business and computers—reigns supreme as the lingua franca, we may as well hurry up and get rid of all the other dialects. This argument assumes that multilingualism is a burden at best, and that having multiple official languages is irrational at worst, impeding a country's competitiveness in the world economy. Lately, however, I've begun to doubt the simplistic rationale behind these arguments.

It is true that a multilingual society brings certain complications with it. Despite having only one official language, Germany is a multilingual society in practice. Recently there has been discussion about many of the children of immigrants not speaking German well enough to keep up at school. There have been articles in the news explaining how this "language problem" was never seriously addressed, in part because experts assumed it would naturally be resolved by the time the second generation, i.e., the children of immigrants, came along. But it wasn't as simple as that. Recent surveys show how, even if these second-generation immigrant children are able to carry on a conversation in German quite fluently, a large percentage of them lack the academic skills necessary to pursue higher education. Conservative pundits have used this to argue that Germany should not admit any immigrants at all—but this viewpoint is clearly misguided, since statistics show that second-generation immigrants in Sweden, for instance, are very academically successful. In other words, the problem isn't with "immigrants" but with Germany's education system. I don't imagine there are any elementary schools in Japan where more than a third of the students do not understand Japanese. That would require a complete overhaul of the existing teacher training programs.

I once read an article in the US that took a more encouraging perspective on the situation, though. It cited a statistic showing that monolingual children tend to perform better than bilingual ones by a small margin, assuming they all study about the same amount. But in cases where bilingual children put slightly more effort into studying, they outperform monolingual children by a huge margin. Of course, I'm not someone who puts blind faith in statistics, nor do I believe that academic ability is something that can be easily quantified and measured. Still, I found the article quite convincing. Although I didn't grow up bilingual, I now live with two languages that coexist in my head. And I'm acutely aware that, if I don't put in a conscious effort to maintain both, my Japanese ability will drop below that of the average Japanese speaker, as will my German, and soon I won't be able to speak either language well at all. On the other hand, when I am exercising and cultivating both languages consciously on a daily basis, they each stimulate the other, giving me a power of expression incomparable to what I had when I could only speak one. When it comes to children, too, it's obvious that being able to speak both Turkish and German is far better than only being able to speak German.

I want to know what a truly multilingual country might make possible: Even if the idea of multilingualism might seem illogical from a purely technical standpoint, we must value the ability to speak and read another language, as well as the daily practice of cultivating this skill. When we value multilingualism, new unforeseen possibilities may open up that do not and cannot exist in a society of solely monolingual speakers. Of course, for that to happen, we would need to spend much more time and money on developing educational and cultural resources. If we fail to do so, then multilingualism, which ought to supply us with such richness of thought and expression, may end up inadvertently shackling us to the past.

Oku Aizu
On the Privilege of Linguistic Immigrants

A FEW YEARS AGO, I WENT ON A TRIP TO OKU AIZU,
a region in the western part of Fukushima, with a few friends of
mine from the publishing world. Mitsuhiro Muroi, a writer and
literary critic from the area, explained to us that the closer you
go to the center of the Japanese archipelago, the spaces between
mountain ranges narrow, and land becomes less flat. As I listened
to him speak, an image suddenly came to mind of Japan as a living
organism with folds and wrinkles. In one of Muroi-san's books, he
also mentions that in Oku Aizu, intonation doesn't really exist in
everyday speech. In "standard" Japanese, if you say the word *hashi*
with an emphasis on the first syllable, it means "chopsticks," but
if you emphasize the second syllable, it means "bridge" or "edge."
Since people in Oku Aizu don't make this distinction, unexpected
possibilities open up: *Tango* could mean "word" or an Argentine
dance. *Samba* could mean a "midwife" or a Brazilian dance.

This reminds me of an accidental connection I once made between the German words *Brücke* (bridge) and *Lücke* (gap, blank)
as a result of my struggle to distinguish between the consonants "r"
and "l." My conflation of these words eventually led me to the idea
that discovering the gaps (*Lücke*) between cultures was much more
interesting than building bridges (*Brücke*) between them. In this
way, two seemingly unrelated words (*tango*) were brought together
by my native phonetic system, and began to *tango* together. From
there, a midwife (*samba*) came along and a new idea was born.
This is the privilege of linguistic immigrants. It is an art that may

seem easy at first glance but is in fact quite difficult to imitate for those who are confined to a single language. Of course some may say, out of spite of course, that I'm simply making puns.

Allegedly, everyone is born with a latent ability to understand and speak any language. This means that acquiring a mother tongue inherently kills off the possibility of speaking any other language at a native level. Experiments have shown that if a child is exposed only to Japanese, it loses the ability to distinguish between "l" and "r" as early as six months of age. Of course, it's not impossible to learn this distinction later in life, but it's certainly not easy. On the other hand, if your mother tongue is a European language, you lose, at least temporarily, the ability to hear inflections in Chinese and other languages, and your ability to memorize Chinese characters becomes progressively slower.

It's amazing to think that a newborn child has the latent ability to speak any language. However, if it maintained this latent ability forever, it would never be able to speak any language at all. To take this conclusion to its logical extreme, we could say that acquiring a mother tongue implies the destruction of all other linguistic possibilities. In a way, it seems a little wasteful.

Perhaps the desire to learn another language as an adult is simply a nostalgic yearning for that time in infancy when we had completely unrestricted movement over our tongue and lips. Reading aloud from a foreign-language textbook as we move our tongue in ways that it usually never moves in everyday life, searching out those places in the mouth where the tongue otherwise never touches—isn't this in essence a kind of dance? Something inside me longs for a tongue that is infinitely flexible, bends in every direction, stretches, shrinks, strikes, and breathes, a tongue that dances about in search of freedom without having to produce a single meaningful sound. But then, of course, no one would understand me. Which is why I'm left with no choice but to pretend I am a rigid monoglot so I can exchange meaningful phrases with people around me. Still, behind this facade is a hidden impulse toward a free tongue.

One summer, I worked as a teaching assistant for an intensive Japanese language course at a university in Hamburg. One of my students told me that his hair had grown out, so he had to go to the hospital. At first I was alarmed. Was hair growth considered an illness in Germany? Then I realized that the student had confused the word hospital (*byoin*) with hairdresser (*biyoin*). They must have sounded indistinguishable to the German student, whereas to me they didn't sound remotely similar. I realized then that many similarities between words are invisible to those who reside inside the language.

Another time, a student told me that there were shops in Hamburg that sold photos and signatures of authors. I was surprised and also somewhat skeptical—I knew that people loved literature in Germany, but a whole store devoted to photos and signatures of authors? As we continued talking, it became clear that the student had meant to say soccer (*sakkā*), not author (*sakka*). Of course, it made perfect sense that there would be stores which sold photographs of soccer games and signatures of soccer players, and that there would be people who would buy such things. Only then did it occur to me that the words for "soccer" and "author" in Japanese must sound quite similar to the student, since the only difference is the length of the final vowel. But to those of us who reside inside the Japanese language, where vowel length is one of the main ways that we differentiate between words, they don't sound the same at all. And since most of us picture Kanji or Katakana to ourselves as we speak, words like "soccer" and "author" are simultaneously "close yet distant," as Sei Shonagon might say. Recently, thanks to the Kanji-conversion errors that often happen when we type, I have more opportunities to notice such coincidences, but it is difficult to notice them when I'm speaking.

In his work, Muroi-san finds connections in the Japanese language that can usually only be seen from the outside, weaving them together to create a strange sort of net. He also has a talent for picking up words and expressions that are only used in specific dialects, cultivating them like seeds in the pages of his writing.

The fields of Oku Aizu weren't as vast as the ones in California, and the landscape was denser. Vegetables grew in small patches here and there. Muroi-san told us that the English word "seminar" is etymologically related to the word "seed," that "fieldwork" too is a kind of work in the fields. It occurred to me that Muroi-san once cotranslated a collection of essays by Seamus Heaney, which led me to wonder: If Ireland uses its distance from the UK as a source of creative energy, perhaps Oku Aizu might do the same with Japan.

But Muroi-san didn't return to Oku Aizu to "discover his roots." There was a period in his life when he worked at a library, and during spare moments at his job, he studied as many different writing systems as possible. Which is to say, it was through the library that he rediscovered the linguistic environment of Oku Aizu. And it was through "fieldwork" that he cultivated this field of his and saw it bear fruit. Those who do this kind of fieldwork are anthropologists of poetry. Muroi-san would go back and forth between the library and the field, reading not only letters but also sounds, objects, soil, and water. He didn't return to his hometown because he was from there, but because some aspect of the culture there interested him. For him, Oku Aizu isn't just a place that provides a sense of belonging, but a plot of land to be continuously cultivated.

We can also dig up sounds in the same way we investigate dialects and words. It's often said that people from Tohoku, the northeast region of Japan, have "heavy mouths." I'd always assumed this "heaviness" meant that they literally couldn't move their mouths quickly or easily. But when I listened to a tape recording from 1976 labeled "Tatsumi Hijikata Butoh Notation," I realized for the first time that this "heaviness" could also refer to a certain rapidity, the way a dropped object gathers speed as it falls.

I noticed that Muroi-san spoke this way, too. Once he opened his mouth, the words would tumble out in a rhythm that seemed to fold in on itself. They wouldn't continue unbroken like a flat board, either. Instead they proceeded bumpily up and down, up and down, like a shovel excavating the layers of air and dirt above and below it.

Basel

How to Cross a Border

ALTHOUGH THE POPULATION OF SWITZERLAND IS A little over half that of Tokyo, it has four official languages: German, French, Italian, and Rhaetian. I don't know if it's because Switzerland is a wealthy country, but whenever Swiss people say that their country has four official languages, it sounds to me like they are bragging about how many expensive accessories they own. If the stereotype about poor people having more children is true, then you would expect that poor countries would have more languages, and rich countries fewer. But when it comes to Switzerland this simply doesn't apply. Unlike Japan, it isn't facing an economic crisis, nor does it have a massive unemployment problem like Germany.

Which is why I was surprised when I once watched an in-flight movie about a Swiss woman who goes to England to work as a maid. The story was only set a hundred years ago, which is not a long time, considering that nowadays it would be practically unheard of for someone to leave Switzerland—a country where jobs are plentiful and well paid—for England, a country famous for its high unemployment rates. In some respects, Switzerland is similar to Japan in that both countries experienced sudden economic growth. When modernization happens quickly, there is a greater chance that old customs and habits will be preserved within the society.

The first time I heard a recording of a cowherd "singing" as he milked his cows in the mountains, I was totally shocked. It seemed to me that only someone who had received daily training from birth in the delicate grammar of animals and had never been exposed to Western music at all could produce a sound like that. What I heard seemed to have no connection to Western musical modes. And yet—this was recorded in Switzerland, smack-dab in the middle of Europe. The recording I listened to was sung by people who lived in the Muota River valley, in Schwyz, a canton of Switzerland. They tend not to like it when their singing is called "yodeling," and it certainly sounded very different from whatever I had heard in standard songbooks. I learned that yodeling is the general term for a style of singing in which vowels are sung in rapid alternation between the chest and head voice, a phenomenon that also exists in Pygmy and Melanesian cultures. It doesn't exist everywhere in Switzerland, and is especially rare in the French-speaking parts. Who was the last person in Europe who could sing like this and when did they live? Unable to get the voice out of my head, I looked it up and discovered that the recording was from 1930. Not so long ago. It would be unthinkable to walk through a meadow nowadays in Schleswig-Holstein and encounter a voice like this. In Tokyo, however, where old and new coexist to a greater degree, you might hear nothing but pop music as you make your way through Shibuya, but set foot in a Noh theater and you'll hear the iconic vocalizations of a Noh actor. The two sounds come from entirely different eras, yet they coexist in the same place at the same time. Japan and Switzerland may be alike in this regard.

Having traveled to many different countries, I think it's not just languages that are different but the way people speak, as well. Everything from the average pitch of voice to the way people vocalize or enunciate can differ depending on the place. When I arrive in Zurich after taking the overnight train from Hamburg, I sometimes feel like I'm in a different universe altogether. Though I've never lived in Switzerland long-term, I followed my PhD advisor, Sigrid Weigel, when she moved from the University of Hamburg to the University of Zurich, which meant that I ended up taking many trips to Zurich, including to turn in my dissertation.

One of the last stops on the train before you arrive in Zurich is Basel. I stayed there once for about three months during the summer of 2001. In German-speaking countries there is a program called *Stadtschreiber* ("city writer"), where a town hosts a writer for a few months and gives them a place to stay along with a stipend to cover their cost of living so that they can have the time and space to write. This is also referred to as an *Aufenthaltsstipendium* (residential scholarship) since it is given to the writer on the condition that they work on-site for a given period of time. The word "scholarship" is often associated with students, but in this case the money goes to a professional writer. The point is for the government to provide direct support to writers, not necessarily to produce literature that sells—and in any case, they have no say over the content of the writer's work. If they did, it would only be indirectly, the way a Japanese publisher or newspaper sometimes influences a writer's work.

Sometimes the program might ask the writer to write something about the town they are staying in; other times, there is no agenda and the writer is simply encouraged to work on whatever project they want. They might be invited to give readings, hold events or colloquiums in the town, speak to high school classes, or talk with the locals, but they're not obligated to do so. They might give an interview in the local newspaper, or their books might be sold in local bookstores. If the writer finishes a book during their residency, they will sometimes mention it in the afterword to the book, along with the date and name of the place where they wrote it, and this is considered an honor for the town that hosted them. Many of the places that have these residential scholarships are small towns that even most German people have never heard of: Wiepersdorf, Scheyern, Edenkoben, for example. There is even one in a suburb of Hamburg called Glückstadt. In fact, it was when I visited Glückstadt almost a decade ago that I first learned that this program existed. The residency in Glückstadt was started by Günter Grass, who donated his former house so that writers could come and stay there.

People often ask me whether a similar program exists in Japan, but I can't think of any. Sometimes a publisher will pay for writers to hole up in a hotel room so that they can finish writing their book—a phenomenon known as "canning." But this is more of a business deal than a cultural program. While I won't go so far as to say that this system never produces quality literature, if I had to guess I would say that in the long term, the "canning" method probably loses out.

In Switzerland, Basel straddles the border of Germany and France, meaning you can essentially walk to either country. It has a thriving cultural scene, especially in literature and the arts. The largest art fair in Europe, Art Basel, is held there every year, and the "House of Literature" is located directly in front of the municipal office. After a woman named Margrit Manz became the director, she began inviting writers to stay in Basel for a few months at a time—though she used the English term "writer-in-residence" rather than *Stadtschreiber*. She also decided to focus on bringing foreign writers who were active in Germany. Before they invited me, they had also invited Aleksandar Tišma, Herta Müller, and Terézia Mora. The term "foreign" here is quite broad, a good illustration of the different ways contemporary writers relate to the German language as well as to the countries surrounding Germany.

Aleksandar Tišma was born in 1924 in what was then called Yugoslavia, and writes in Serbo-Croatian. He neither lives in Germany nor writes in German, but has vastly more readers there than in his home country. As a result, he is constantly coming to Germany for talks and readings. Though his German is quite good, he has never written anything in German. There are actually quite a few writers who fall into this category, including a writer from Denmark named Inger Christensen, whose work I love, as well as a Dutch writer named Cees Nooteboom whose work has been translated into Japanese.

Herta Müller is from Romania but speaks German as her mother tongue. Born in 1953 in a German-speaking Romanian village called Nitzkydorf, she studied German and Southern European literature, then worked as a translator and teacher, but eventually lost her job when she refused to cooperate with the secret police. She seems to have bided her time by working at a preschool for a while before moving to Germany in 1987. There is still a German-speaking minority in Romania, and many German-language Romanian writers besides Herta Müller to whom whole literary festivals are dedicated. In a way, the popularity of literature from German-speaking regions of Eastern Europe hasn't changed much since Kafka's time.

Terézia Mora was born in Hungary in 1971. She witnessed the fall of the Berlin Wall and lived through perestroika. She later moved to Germany (although not as a refugee) and still writes novels in German to this day.

These examples show that there are many ways for literature to cross borders. Sometimes people leave their countries but not their mother tongue, while sometimes they leave their country as well as their mother tongue behind.

Though I never set foot outside the German language while I was staying in Basel, there were a few instances in which it felt like I had. Although the language spoken in Switzerland is technically German, it can be difficult for people from Germany to understand it, even after several months of living there. Some even say that you may never fully understand it. This is somewhat similar to the way a mainland Japanese person might experience Okinawa. The novelist Karl-Heinz Ott, who is from the Swabian region of Germany and lives in Freiburg, talks about how he worked in theaters in Zurich and Basel for many years, and always assumed he had a thorough understanding of Swiss German. But one day, he got into an argument with someone and realized he didn't understand everything that was being said. Of course, standards for "understanding" and "not understanding" can vary depending on the person. Whereas an average person might think they have "completely understood" something, a writer might have a tendency to overly scrutinize a situation and exaggerate the parts they don't understand. In any case, his anecdote showed me that Swiss German can be hard to understand even for native German speakers from Germany.

Though Swiss German was on the decline about thirty or forty years ago, since then there has been a movement to revive it and it has made something of a comeback. It's clear that Swiss people view their German with pride. During my residency, I went on many excursions in the mountains of Graubünden. Sometimes people who spoke to me on the train didn't speak standard German, but did speak English. I thought that if they could speak English so well, it would surely be easy enough for them to learn standard German. But they were very reluctant to do so. When I told my Swiss friends in Basel about this, they explained that if a Swiss German person learned standard German, the only people they'd be able to talk to would be Germans and Austrians. So, it made sense for them to speak Swiss German at home and English everywhere else.

Even within Switzerland, there are different dialects across regions. People say that if you cross one mountain range you'll hear what sounds like a completely different language. So when I say "Swiss German" I am referring to a common language born out of many different dialects. In that sense, Swiss German is not really a dialect, but many Germans refer to it that way.

But there are still many actual dialects that exist within Germany. Go to any of the rural areas and you'll hear no shortage of Bavarian or Swabian. There are plenty of German people even of my generation who speak standard German in their everyday lives but dialect with their families. But Swiss German is different from a "dialect" in this sense. I still remember when Adolf Muschg, a literature professor at ETH Zurich, invited me to his university to give a talk, and I heard him speaking with another professor in Swiss German. In German universities, professors would never speak in dialect with each other, even if they were from the same region.

I once read an article by a Swiss writer where they discussed how some people doubted whether serious subjects like politics, economics, or the natural sciences could be debated in Swiss German without sounding unnatural. The writer derided these comments as ignorant. After all, Swiss German is not just a dialect limited to the private sphere—it is an official language actively used in politics and academia. More than anything else, though, it is also a language that asserts itself against High German.

At the same time, the existence of Swiss German also poses a barrier to communication with French- and Italian-speaking people in Switzerland. When a literary festival is held in Basel or Zurich, it is only German-speaking Swiss people who come, while those who speak French usually go to Paris. And since Swiss literature is written in multiple languages, there isn't a strong sense of national literary identity—which means that, when it comes to literature, Switzerland has many borders within the borders of its own country. And then of course there are the invisible economic borders between the German-speaking regions of Switzerland, which tend to be affluent and conservative, and the regions where other languages are spoken. When Switzerland was denied entry into the European Economic Community because of opposition from the German-speaking Swiss population, the French-speaking people chained themselves to chairs in the roads in protest. In this way, what was once an invisible border within the country was temporarily rendered perceptible. The German-speaking regions of Switzerland want to become independent so that they can have the upper hand economically, while the French-speaking regions want to lower restrictions for working in France.

Basel was an easy place to live. Though foreigners make up only 10 percent of the German population, in Switzerland that number is much higher, and I'd regularly see young men of Indian or African descent in town. Perhaps it was just my imagination, but they seemed to be at ease there. There wasn't the usual tension you feel in Germany. No one looked like a neo-Nazi, and it was obvious that the people from the town weren't threatened by the presence of foreigners either. Staying there was pleasant. But when I would try to listen to the conversations of people around me while waiting for the train, I often had no idea what they were saying, since they were speaking Swiss German. In that sense, I sometimes felt perplexed by the contrast between the sense of openness exhibited toward the world at large, and its insularity within the rest of Europe.

Seoul

Enforced Exophony

IN MARCH OF 2011 I WENT TO SEOUL, AGAIN INVITED by the Goethe Institute. Koreans seem to hold Germany and German culture in high regard, to the point that Korea has the largest number of German studies scholars in the world outside of Germany—although I've also heard that that number has been declining in recent years.

Zsuzsanna Gahse was there from Germany, and Sabine Scholl from Switzerland, as well Michael Böhler from Austria. The theme of the conference was "transculture," and included readings, symposiums, lectures, and workshops with students over the course of several days.

Whenever I'm invited to Eastern Europe or the US as a German-language author, I always jump at the opportunity. But when the same invitation came from Seoul, I hesitated. I worried they'd be disappointed when they saw I was Japanese, as they might be expecting a German scholar instead. But that worry turned out to be unfounded. The Korean scholars, writers, playwrights, and students were all eager to engage. We mostly spoke in German, but it was different from other contexts. I felt a genuine sense of warmth from my interlocutors. We debated each other, had dinner together, walked to the conference room together, waited for the bus together. I was moved by the simple fact of our hearts and minds and bodies being there, passing time together in this way. I even felt sad when it came time to leave, something I usually never feel when I travel somewhere for work. Seoul was the only exception.

During one panel discussion, a student in the audience asked the author Park Wan-suh which foreign writers she had been most influenced by. She rattled off a list of European names, including Dostoyevsky and Balzac. The student raised their hand again, looking puzzled. "You weren't influenced by any Japanese authors?" This time it was Park Wan-suh's turn to look surprised. "Didn't you just ask me which foreign authors I've been influenced by? People of my generation never considered Japanese literature foreign because we were forced to read in Japanese. We weren't allowed to read in Korean. I read Dostoyevsky and Balzac and all the other European writers in Japanese."

Suddenly, a dark shadow fell over the word "exophony." I realized how it sounded for me, a Japanese person, to be harping on about the joys of venturing outside one's mother tongue—particularly here in Korea, where Japan had forced the Korean people into an exophonic condition against their will. People have no right to proselytize about the joys of exophony if they have never been forced to speak in a language not their own.

I wondered if part of the reason that the idea of linguistic purity has been so important to Korea is because of their geopolitical position, sandwiched between China, a cultural giant, and Japan, their former colonizer. After all, Koreans have tried to abolish Chinese characters in their writing system. "Won't it be difficult to read older texts if you abolish Chinese characters?" I asked at one point in the conference. "Maybe, but we can't keep using Chinese characters if we want to curb the influence of Chinese culture on our own." It was true—as long as Korea continued using Chinese characters, they would never be able to get out from under the shadow of Chinese culture.

I felt torn. On the one hand, I don't believe in linguistic or cultural purity. That would be delusional. On the other hand, I do think the Japanese language has too many loanwords. I don't know if taking a laissez-faire approach to language is always wise. After all, loanwords don't just randomly enter a language; someone, somewhere consciously decides to add them. If there were a movement to regulate the amount of loanwords coming into Japanese every year, would I be for or against it? France now regulates the official number of English loanwords that can be used in French. In comparison, it sometimes feels like every other word in Japanese is a loanword. It reminds me of a cramped, one-bedroom apartment overflowing with random junk because its occupant keeps going on impulsive shopping sprees. Isn't it better not to buy things we don't need?

And yet, sentences like the following have become entirely normal these days: "The latest SEASON of our TOTAL LIFESTYLE BRAND series DEBUTS its second COLLECTION at our newly OPENED Marunouchi location. PERFECT for stylish young women! Presenting SIMPLE, elegant STYLES using high quality materials, such as black SHEEP LEATHER SHIRTS, stylish VELVET SUITS, COATS, and DRESSES with wide, DRAPING collars." There seems to be a high concentration of Katakana loanwords when it comes to taking about consumer goods, which always come equipped with their own special adjectives and which are also loanwords. The marketing professionals must be betting on the stupidity of their consumers, who often have no idea what these words mean.

At one point in time, Japanese had its own, perfectly functioning words for pants: *zubora*, *suppon*, for example. But now people just call them "pantsu." I don't really care when department stores use this word, but novels? Why novels have to follow the logic of department stores is beyond me.

Some Japanese writers, like Taeko Tomioka, use Katakana in a purposeful, self-conscious way. Tomioka uses Katakana to render words that are normally written in Hiragana or Kanji, which has a defamiliarizing effect on the reader. The words become less weighty, more mysterious, taking on an almost shamanistic quality. In her novel *Building Waves*, she writes the word *katagi*, which means "respectable," in Katakana rather than Kanji, and suddenly the word is released from its chains of obligation. Similarly, the word *tsukkendon* (curt), usually written in Kanji, looks like an onomatopoeia when written in Katakana. Sometimes she'll even write ordinary words and phrases like *suteki* (lovely) or *sukiyo* (I like you) in Katakana, which has the effect of elevating them from their otherwise mundane status. And when she writes the names of body parts like *atama* (head), *futomomo* (thigh), *hentosen* (tonsils) in Katakana, they look like they belong to androids rather than human beings:

頭　　　アタマ

太もも　フトモモ

扁桃腺　ヘントウセン

Katakana becomes a tool for bringing old things back to life again, rather than promoting flashy new loanwords to sell consumer goods. Reading Tomioka reminds me that we can't just eliminate Katakana because loanwords are unpleasant. Instead we must push them to their fullest, most radical potential. There is simply no other option.

Katakana is not the only "foreign" orthography used in Japanese novels these days. In *An I-Novel* Minae Mizumura writes in both English and Japanese. But these days, even in mainstream Japanese-language books, it has become almost impossible not to use English in some way, especially when it comes to words like "CD" or "T-shirt." I do think it's interesting to consciously include words written in English this way, but I have a strong aversion to using English to write regular words like "CD" or "T-shirt." This might have something to do with the fact that I've lived in Germany for so long. When my German-speaking friends look at the books I've written in Japanese, it bothers me that these are the only words they can read. That's why I decided that none of my characters will ever wear T-shirts or listen to CDs anymore. It's actually quite inconvenient. The other option, of course, would be to double down and use even more English words, so that pointless words like T-shirt and CD won't stand out as much.

If Japan hadn't committed war crimes against Korea—or had at least taken responsibility for them—perhaps linguistic exchange would feel more possible. As it is, however, writing about Korea is difficult. I've found I can write more easily about a place that doesn't have as much to do with Japan. That is probably why I was finally able to start writing this book only after I'd gone to Senegal. I could be more irresponsible when writing about Senegal. But with Korea, I feel responsible—to the point that whatever I write about it feels like self-deception. This isn't just about language. If someone asked me my impressions of Korea, I would honestly say that I felt a sense of warmth and intellectual curiosity from the people there. Whenever other Japanese people go to other Asian countries on holiday, I have to restrain myself from letting out a sarcastic laugh when they make breezy comments like, "It was so fun!" or "The weather was so nice!" And yet here I am, doing the same exact thing.

In June of 2002, the University of Trier held a symposium comparing representations of Turkish people in German media to representations of other Asian people in Japanese media. I learned that there has been a recent increase in representations of other Asian people on Japanese TV. Often, the Japanese media heavily idealizes them. They'll say things like: "These Asian people have a warmth and vitality that Japanese people lost long ago" or "These are people that really value their friendships and family ties." At the same time, there is rampant prejudice against immigrants of Asian descent in Japan. Japanese people will claim that they came here "illegally," that they steal or have ties to the mafia. But this idealizing and demonizing are two sides of the same medal—which is highly inconvenient to the winner.

In Europe, too, there have always been two parallel images of people considered outside the purview of European civilization: one of "barbarians," seen as cruel and frightening, and the other of pure innocent people. Europeans could then affirm their own humanity by telling themselves that they were neither of those things. Japanese people do something similar. By describing other Asian people as "latecomers to civilization who still possess the warmth we lost long ago," they reassure themselves that they are cold, intellectual, civilized—unlike those "other" Asian people who are the opposite. In other words, rather than acknowledging the historical reality of their own colonial invasions, destruction, and murder, by labeling other Asian people as "warm" and "compassionate," Japanese people can thereby suppress the consciousness and memory of their own crimes.

At the airport in Seoul, the departures and arrivals board displayed a list of flights bound for Tokyo. I glanced at the timetable as I boarded my flight for Paris. I wouldn't be stopping in Japan on my way back this time—something that filled me with a strange mixture of sadness and relief.

Vienna

Rejecting the Language of Immigrants

I LOVE GOING TO AUSTRIA BECAUSE WRITERS ARE treated so well there, regardless of how many books they've sold (unlike how it is in Japan). In fact, in Austria, the fewer books you've sold, the more respected you are. But this only applies when you are with people who work in the arts. As soon as you set foot in the city, it's a different story.

One time, I was leaving the Kunsthistorisches Museum in Vienna in a good mood when I noticed my camera battery was dead. Thinking I'd buy a new one, I set out to cross the Ring, but twisted my ankle as I was rushing to cross the street before the light changed. I was lucky there were no cars coming at the time. Dragging my sprained ankle behind me, I made my way to a bench on the sidewalk facing the lawn and sat down, only to find that it was covered with swastikas. I felt sorry for myself, but there were no other benches available. Plus, my ankle was too sore for me to walk, so I had no choice but to stay where I was. It was the picture of irony. Was I sitting on a bench covered in swastikas because I'm from a country that allied itself with the Nazis, or because I had a non-Aryan face—which, in present-day Austria, meant I could very well be targeted? Did I feel a sense of relief knowing that for once, I was on the side of the oppressed, rather than the oppressor? In any case, the whole thing was a miserable caricature.

For several years now, far-right political parties in Europe have been garnering votes on anti-immigration platforms. Every time it seems to be abating, the trend comes back again in full force, and sometimes it feels like the whole shoreline will be inundated. Austria is one of these countries. When I was invited to the "March literature" festival in 2002, it was the first time I'd been to Vienna in over a year. Everyone was talking about a new immigration law that had just passed, which stipulated that all foreigners who had been in Austria for a certain number of years would be required to take a German language exam. If they failed, they would be deported. I had never heard of anything like this.

Without much context, you might think the policy is simply instilling a respect for language. However, unless they are especially interested in language learning, most adults who come to a foreign country to work are too busy to study the language properly. In Germany, the government pays for asylum seekers and refugees to attend a language school for the first few months after their arrival. I think framing language study as a right is a good thing. Language study as obligatory I can more or less get behind. But being deported if you fail a language exam? That can't be understood as anything but an excuse for deporting foreigners. Exophony is a right of all immigrants, but not an obligation. It's especially heinous to force people who have had to flee their own country to abandon their mother tongue and speak a different one. Accepting a refugee means accepting every part of them, language and all.

But the deeper problem with this policy is that it's an attempt to eliminate "incorrect" mother tongues. The conservative party in Austria, represented by Haider and others like him, are even rejecting modern art as "decadent" because it is useless to the masses. This is the same policy that the Nazis had. I have noticed that although experimental literature is popular in Austria, the gap between the aesthetic views of the literati and so-called reg-ular"people seems bigger than it is in Germany, where everyone more or less shares a political consciousness around war responsibility. Which explains why, even though experimental writing is not as popular in Germany as it is in Austria, a wider swath of the reading public seems willing to engage in contemporary literature, even if it is slightly difficult or challenging.

Every time I go to Austria, I am viscerally reminded that literary people have almost no relationship to "ordinary" citizens. I could be reading some nearly incomprehensible prose poetry at a reading for over an hour, and no one would bat an eye, since only people who are already interested in this kind of thing would be in attendance anyway. In Germany the readership is much wider, so all kinds of people come to my readings, but if I read an incomprehensible prose poem someone would likely interrupt me and say something like: "How do you expect to stop the impending war writing such out-of-touch stories?" or "How do you think literature will respond to the next terrorist attack?" Sometimes I get fed up with the overly political Germans and long for Austria, but then I remember that the current situation in Austria is quite dangerous, as it is similar to that of Germany in the 1930s. Avant-garde and experimental art in 1930s Germany was much more interesting than what exists now—and yet, their society descended into fascism and no one could do anything to stop it.

Recently, I listened to a radio play by Ernst Jandl called *The Humanists*. Jandl was an Austrian poet and a master of wordplay who died in 2000. Few authors could draw as big of a crowd as he could. On average, thirty to fifty people might come to a literary reading, perhaps a hundred if it's a festival, but Jandl's readings would regularly draw over three hundred. His work was just that delightful to the ear.

In *The Humanists*, the author deliberately juxtaposes the expressive speech of migrant laborers with the fascistic language of those who deem this "bad German." He does not claim that the language of migrant workers is inherently "good," but shows how language must first break down in order to take on new life, and that we cannot leave this reconstitution to historical chance. Instead, art must be broken artistically. Some people might think that wordplay is just a way to kill time. I think it contains an expressive potential that the oppressed can grasp and wield for their own purposes.

Hamburg
Seeking the Voice

THOUGH I LIVE IN HAMBURG, I RARELY GET TO spend time here as I'm often traveling to other cities. Typically I write on the train or in hotels. Sometimes I'll have a stretch of ten days or so when I'm not traveling, and I realize how nice it is to be at home. Is Hamburg the most interesting city in Europe? It's difficult to say. Berlin is probably more interesting. But there's no doubt Hamburg is a special place to me. I've lived here ever since I moved to Germany in 1982, so when I walk around the city, it appears to me like a palimpsest of memories from different periods of my life, such as when I was a student or a company employee.

Recently, there are more and more people like me who live transient lives, frequently moving from one city to another. I once came across a survey in a magazine where a number of such peripatetics were asked what makes a city feel like home. "When I know my dentist and barber," someone said. "When I have a bicycle there," another one responded. That really resonated with me.

When I'm at home, I write in the mornings. In the afternoon I usually go for a walk, or do errands. Sometimes I just listen to the radio or a CD and space out—though I tend to listen to recordings of literary readings more than to music.

These days, more and more bookstores have started carrying CDs. In addition to audiobooks of classics, they also have spoken poetry, radio dramas, authors reading their own work, and even collaborations between writers and musicians. I like listening to experimental voice art. It used to be much bigger back in the days of the Fluxus movement, and whenever I listen to something by Jaap Blonk, the whole atmosphere of that time comes flooding back to me.

The Blonk recording is from the seventies, but the poems by Hugo Ball that he references are much older, from 1916. The highlight of the recording is when Blonk reads Tristan Tzara's poem "BRÜLLT" ("Bellow"), a word he repeats a total of 410 times. In German, the "b" and "r" sounds have a terrifyingly explosive quality to them, and from the first time Blonk yells "BRÜLLT" it already sounds like he is injuring his throat, but just when you think he has reached his limit, he keeps going, and you begin to feel you can't take it anymore, and secretly wish the performance would end, but you keep holding out, half afraid and unable to turn off the recording, and all the while Blonk shows no sign of letting up, bellowing with such force that it sounds like his body might split in two, to the point you're convinced that if he keeps going he is definitely going to die—but still it doesn't end. Every time I listen to it, I'm reminded of how awe-inspiring a thing the human voice is. It also makes me think how comical it is that we go around saying the words "yell," "scream," and "shout" in a flat, normal tone without really thinking about it.

While extreme readings like these are interesting to listen to, there are also quieter, but no less memorable ones. When I listen to recordings of the Danish poet Inger Christensen reading her poems I feel like they're casting a spell on me. Or people like Barbara Köhler or Oskar Pastior—there's nothing flashy about their readings, but the wordplay in their poems stands out more when they're read aloud, to the point that they evoke different images than when I'm reading them on the page. When read aloud, poetry becomes a form of incantation, prayer, conversation, performance, speech, song.

Listening to the many different voices and languages playing over the speakers calls to mind the word "native speaker." When I was in junior high and high school in Japan, we would sometimes have to listen to recordings of "native speakers" in English class to improve our pronunciation. These recordings would always be played on tape recorders. Thus, in my mind, the "native speaker" was always associated with a machine. Maybe that is why, to this day, I'm struck by how strange it is that a human voice can reach us from so far away. The worse the quality of the machine, the better. I especially like when the voice can only be heard in fits and starts, in a kind of low, mumbling static.

In language learning, I used to think that grammar was something you learned on the page, in a textbook, and that conversation was learned through listening to a native speaker. But that no longer seems true to me. Grammar, too, is closely related to the voice. Children learn grammar before they learn the alphabet. Key grammatical elements, like word order, separable verbs, and articles are intuited at the level of rhythm and music. Adults do this too, to a certain extent. Sometimes it feels like a sentence is missing something, an absence about the size of an eighth note, perhaps, and, unless it is filled with an article or something else, the rhythm of the phrase feels off.

There is a Swedish linguist named Bengdt Sandberg who once read an essay of mine that had to do with the German word *es* (which is roughly equivalent to the English word *it*) and kindly sent me a book of his on the topic. What I was grappling with was why *es* is sometimes used in odd ways that semantics cannot account for. Sandberg explained that when you create a sentence on the basis of meaning alone, there are sometimes gaps left over that must be filled in with something. The word *es* fulfills this function of a placeholder, similar to a rest in musical notation. Obviously I am oversimplifying what I'm sure is a complex topic within the field of linguistics but—speaking from personal experience—I can definitely relate to the feeling that a sentence is missing something, and needs an extra word to fill it out.

Which means that when children, and to a certain extent adults, read out loud, they are internalizing the rules of grammar.

Another important aspect of grammar is emotion. This is another way in which grammar is similar to music. I have a pretty bad memory, and have always struggled to memorize new words. However, I have discovered that if I say a word out loud while I am having a strong emotional reaction to something, it sticks in my memory immediately. If I say a word when I am extremely angry I will never forget it. I also tend to remember a word if someone says something to me that makes me happy. When the heart is moved, the word is imprinted in the memory.

Children are quite volatile emotionally and often lack the tools for managing their feelings. When they want something they really want it, and when they are sad they cry right away. Maybe the fact that they feel their emotions so intensely gives them an advantage when it comes to memorizing words.

In Japanese, it is difficult to remember the rules for the "te" form of a verb. I remember how much my students struggled with this back when I used to teach Japanese. Why does the word *kaku* (to write) become *kaite* in the "te" form, while *kau* (to buy) becomes *katte*? It seemed remarkable to me that a small child could memorize such a difficult conjugation with ease. But upon further thought, I realized that children have ample opportunity to learn the "te" form because it is used to make imperatives. When they say things like *Ne, kore katte!* ("Hey, buy me this!") or *Are yatte!* ("Do that!") they must be internalizing the "te" form. It's not that they first learn the infinitive of the verb and then its variant. Instead, they memorize the variant itself. Then, as years go by, they begin to use the "te" form in the conjunctive sense, as when schoolgirls talk to each other, although it never quite loses its infantile melody: *Dakara ano fuku kattē, kitemitē, kiniiranakutē, mata mise ni modottē*... ("So, like, I bought this shirt, and then I tried it on at home, but then I didn't like it, and then I had to like return it...")

When I'm in my house at night, I often listen to the radio. I only watch TV about once a month at most. I find the images on TV in particular unbearably cringey, and the language completely unstimulating. It's like a rug being shaken out and the dust flying everywhere—sensational, but completely unoriginal.

The national radio station, on the other hand, is quite substantial. They broadcast radio plays, documentaries, literary criticism, theater reviews—they talk about upcoming art exhibits and even compare how different newspapers report on the same events. They also broadcast readings of literary works and interview contemporary musicians about their work. My favorite station is Radio Deutschland in Berlin. In the past, broadcasting programs in northern Germany were very good, but recently, perhaps due to funding cuts, the content has become quite shallow and they mostly just play albums. In Germany, radio stations are an important part of literary life.

Reading poetry or fiction requires an ability to listen to words and conjure images in your head as you read. I think radio maximizes the power of words to bring images to life through our sense of hearing. Maybe that's why people who like reading books generally tend to like listening to the radio, and why those same people usually dislike TV.

Since I first moved to Hamburg in 1982, my ears have completely changed. Though I had studied German in Japan, I had almost no listening comprehension skills when I arrived. I could read a fairly difficult book with the help of a dictionary, and I had a decent grasp of German grammar and vocabulary, so I could basically say what I wanted to say. But I couldn't understand what other people were saying to me. Mine was the opposite situation to that of infants, who can understand much of what is said to them but cannot speak or read. When I spoke, my sentences were grammatically correct, but they had no musicality, since I was constructing them based on logic alone. But over time, I started to understand what people were saying, and eventually their words flowed easily into my ears. That didn't happen because I was learning individual words and phrases, but because I began to grasp the whole language in a musical way.

Being attuned to the musicality of language can tell us a lot. If a person's pitch is suspended, it means a sentence is not yet concluded. Similarly, rhythmic breaks punctuate distinct units of meaning. The main clause has its own melody, as does the subordinate clause. Certain words may be emphasized—for example, the speaker might slow down—indicating that the meaning of the sentence is concentrated there, while less important words are passed over more quickly. In other words, the structure of a sentence is expressed in its melody, and if you listen in a musical way, you'll have a blueprint for navigating a large and complex building.

Perhaps venturing outside your mother tongue means surrendering yourself to a different kind of music.

If you live in the same place for many years, you begin to talk like a "native speaker" and over time you may even lose your accent. But losing your accent isn't the goal of learning a language. In fact, it's important not to lose sight of the value of accents. In *Japanese and Creole*, Katsuhiko Tanaka says: "Not only speech, but also thought must have its own accent ... *to accent* is to contribute, however modestly, to the philosophy of the world and the culture of humanity."

Recently I was taking the train back to Hamburg. The window was open, and though it was summer, a chilly wind blew in. The passenger next to me asked if I wanted it closed, which led to us chatting about the weather and exchanging a few pleasantries. At one point, they expressed surprise that I didn't have an accent, and

I couldn't help laughing a little. Whenever I'm talking in a casual setting about something unimportant, my accent disappears. But if I'm talking about something serious and have to think hard about what I'm going to say, my accent comes out again. When I'm reading something I've written in public, my accent actually becomes an important structural element of the rhythm of my language.

Writing literature is the opposite of regurgitating the language we hear in our everyday lives. It is to come face-to-face with the very brink of language and its possibilities. When you do, the well-worn grooves in your memory may be reinvigorated as the old layers of your mother tongue deform the language you currently use.

That is why, when I write in German, I search for the rhythm that resonates with me, and when I read it aloud, I consciously distance myself from so-called natural, everyday usages of the language. People will often tell me that they have no trouble understanding me, but that there's something about my use of German that's not "normal." What they are hearing is the accumulation of sound that I, as an individual, have absorbed over the course of my existence in this multilingual world. It is meaningless to try and lose my accent or habits of speech. If anything, human beings in the modern world are repositories for countless languages that unmake and undo one another. Attempts to eliminate that mutual distortion are ultimately futile. We might even go so far as to say that the act of literary creation simply amounts to pursuing the consequences of one's accent.

There was a period of about six months or so when I was seeing a specialist in Hamburg for my accent. Most of their job consisted of working with actors on how to suppress their accent at will. First they conducted a thorough analysis of my speech patterns, which revealed that on the whole, I spoke in a very flat, even tone, without much variation in word emphasis. The analysis also revealed that whenever I would try to emphasize a particular word, I would simply raise my intonation. This is fairly standard for people whose mother tongue is Japanese. In German, when you say the sentence "I went to Berlin yesterday," the word "Berlin" is emphasized. If the time when the person went to Berlin is the most important piece of information, then the word "yesterday" will be emphasized. In German, however, unlike Japanese, placing emphasis on a word does not mean raising the pitch of your voice. Instead, the accented syllables of the emphasized word are said more strongly and slowly, while the other words are said quickly and weakly. If you speak this way in Japanese, you will sound unrefined, since it is better to speak unhurriedly, and emphasize all words equally, with the same intensity and speed.

My favorite word in German and the one I always like to put emphasis on is *nicht* ("not" in English). Barring special circumstances, this is a word that you normally don't emphasize. It sounds over the top if you do, since it's a word that turns the rest of the sentence on its head, which means it naturally comes to the fore. But unfortunately, it is one of the only words that brings me great joy to say with emphasis.

When I think about the particularities of my "accent" in this way, I realize that it has an inseparable connection to my writing style. Each word follows the preceding one in an endless stream, without hierarchy, with only the gesture of negation leaping up in joy. Rather than "correct" this quirk of mine, I intentionally polish and develop it.

I also discovered another interesting tendency when analyzing my accent. In Japanese, the "b" sound that is formed by the upper and lower lips coming together is not as strong as the "b" sound in German, which means that generally my "plosives" are much weaker than the average German speaker's. Similarly, the "n" sound in Japanese requires the speaker to close the back of their throat, whereas in German, the speaker has to push the tongue against their palate, making the sound more open. So when you analyze them closely, words that at first sound identical turn out to be entirely different. Those who can hear it hear it, and those who can't can't. I work hard to attune my ears to these subtle differences in sound, the same way an actor might. But that's not because I'm ashamed of my accent. It's because I want to better understand these elements that lie outside the sonic environment in which I was raised. I am trying to learn, with my tongue, sounds that are unfamiliar to me. A foreign-sounding word learned out of curiosity is not "imitation" per se. All of these things I learn leave traces that slowly grow to coexist with my accent. And that balancing act never really stabilizes, but goes on changing indefinitely.

Recently I met an opera singer in Hanover who told me she still went to a voice teacher from time to time, even though she has been a professional for many years. She said it helped her have an outside perspective on her own vocal techniques, since she is constantly developing new habits throughout her singing career. I have a similar experience with reading my work out loud. Suddenly I'll find I'm unable to do something that I had previously done with ease. Something I had taken great pains to learn will start to sound distorted. But sometimes, out of the blue, I realize I have learned to do something I thought I would never be able to do, without my noticing. When you live with two languages in your head, the balance between the two never fully stabilizes. It's possible the system of sounds we produce is constantly changing.

Gainesville
World Literature, Reconsidered

IN THE SPRING OF 2002, I GAVE A LECTURE AT THE University of Florida in Gainesville. Afterward, someone asked me what I thought about the distinction between "Japanese literature" and "world literature." The person who asked the question seemed to have some familiarity with Japan, where this is a common way of categorizing books. I never thought anything of it when I lived there, but it now struck me as odd. After all, separating "Japanese literature" from "world literature" implies that Japan is not a part of the world—that "the world" is something outside of Japan.

This is not quite how things are done in Germany. For example, my *Dictionary of Modern German Literature* categorizes its entries "German-language literature" and "foreign-language literature." Not "Japan" and "the world" but "German language" and "foreign language." Using "German literature" would have excluded writers from Austria and Switzerland, as well as Turkish and Czech writers who write in German. This still posed a problem for me, however, since I write in both German and Japanese. When I asked the editor of the dictionary which category I should be listed under, they said they supposed I should be listed under both. All borders exist in order to be crossed.

Recently, an anthology of Japanese literature was published in Russia. There were two volumes in this anthology. One was titled *OH* ("him" in Russian) which contained only works by male authors, and the other *OHA* ("her") which contained only works by female authors. This is another way to categorize literature, one that Japanese bookstores often use as well. It reminds me of my student days at the University of Hamburg, when the idea of "women's writing" was being fiercely debated. But the Russian anthology of Japanese literature wasn't forwarding any kind of theory of gender and writing. It was more akin to how a department store divides their clothing into "men's" and "women's" sections. Recently there was a series published in China called New Works by Chinese and Japanese Women Writers. It would have been interesting if the series had completely rejected national categories in favor of gender, but all they did was add the qualifier "Japan" to "woman."

The whole academic debate about women's literature being different from men's literature and gender being different from biological sex eventually led to the conclusion that even works by male authors could fall under the category of "women's literature." (At that point we had decided that all our favorite authors were women, be they Kleist or anyone else.) But just when we thought we had gotten to the bottom of things, people began to argue that the question of "biological sex" couldn't be completely ignored either. Eventually I came to the conclusion that while both sex and gender were part of the equation, in neither case did it delimit what an author could write.

In Germany, there is yet another category called "immigrant literature," which I am sometimes included in because I have written books in German. In interviews, I'm often asked how I feel about being called an immigrant writer, and whether it bothers me to be defined that way. In Japan, interviewers sometimes ask how I feel about being referred to as a *joryu sakka*—a woman writer. Nowadays the more common term is *josei sakka*, but I wonder if the "ryu" in *joryu* is a more appropriate description of gender, since the character means flow, current, or stream in addition to style or mode. The "sei" in *josei* means sex, indicating a set of characteristics you were born with, but "ryu" describes doing something in a particular way or method. A method is not permanent. There is no need to stick with it. You can wash it away any time you like. Maybe one person is taught that a "woman" is a particular kind of thing, and that is how they happen to be going about it, but another person might decide that that mode of womanhood is uninteresting and choose a different one. In that sense, perhaps when we use the term *joryu bungaku*, or women's literature, what we're describing is writing by a person who is existing in a womanly "mode" or "way." To use the term *josei bungaku* implies some innate characteristic I was born with, which doesn't seem right. The term takes itself far too seriously.

In North America, it's common to foreground the issue of race in a way that's less common in Germany. Once, I was invited to a literary festival in Canada, and was surprised to find myself listed in their program under "Literature of Color." At first I thought it was describing my work as colorful, but apparently it was referring to literature written by people of color. These included writers of African and Asian descent, and I was asked to speak as a writer from this category. It made sense in the North American context, where social problems stem from the divisions between white people and people of color, but it maps less neatly onto the German context. Foreigners in Germany who are targeted by neo-Nazis include Russian returnees, Polish, Jewish, Italian, and Spanish people, as well as people from the former Yugoslavia. All of them are technically white. Of course there are also incidents in which African, Turkish, and Vietnamese people are attacked too, but still, the stark division between white people and people of color does not make as much sense in the German context.

There are more unique ways of categorizing literature. A few years ago, there was a multiday literary festival in Berlin whose theme was "sex." The first day was about "Heterosexual Literature," the second was about "Homosexual Literature," the third on "Fetishes and Sadomasochism," and the fourth was simply called "Other." I was invited to read on the fourth night, probably because I am an animist who experiences objects, trees, and letters as erotic. On the night before the festival, someone called the venue and asked: "What kinds of things do people in the 'Other' category do?"

Weimar
Small Languages, Big Languages

IN 1999, I WENT TO WEIMAR FOR THE 250TH ANNI-versary of Goethe's birth. They invited me to be part of a panel on the concept of "world literature," which Goethe came up with, and asked me to talk about what I thought world literature meant in the twenty-first century. The first thing that came to mind was translated literature. I wasn't interested in thinking about world literature as opposed to national literatures, but I was interested in the way words change when they cross national borders. So I talked about how world literature might be understood as trans-lated literature, since the only way we can access "world literature" at all is through translation. Translation is often thought of as a necessary evil. And although the question of translation had rarely been considered in relation to literature more broadly, I decided to proceed from the idea that world literature was first and foremost translated literature.

Durs Grünbein and Ingo Schulze, both young German writers, were on the panel, as well as Ben Okri and Yang Lian, from Nigeria and China, both of whom live in London.

Ben Okri said that he couldn't count the number of times peo-ple had asked him: "Isn't it impossible to depict the real Africa in English? Shouldn't you be writing in your local language instead?" I agreed that that was a strange question. English is a language that constantly absorbs different elements into itself, and besides, there are many different Englishes. The whole premise of the question suggests that English can only describe things that happen in England. You can't decide in advance what any particular language is suited to describing. Besides, there is no such thing as "the real Africa"—there are infinite ways of experiencing Africa, grasping it, and expressing it. It would be ridiculous to ask which authors are depicting the "real" Germany, and the fact that people simply look at a developing country and immediately think there is some "objective" reality there to be described is absurd. The words we use and the things we describe have infinite faces. And of course, there are many faces that have yet to be discovered.

But I sensed that the question directed at Ben Okri, which includes a tacit criticism of African writers who write in English, also implies something else: that he should be "saving" the minor languages on the verge of extinction. In other words, the writer is made to bear the role of an ambulance, rushing to rescue endangered languages. Languages disappearing or being forgotten is certainly not a new phenomenon, but only in the last century or so has there been a concerted effort to put them on life support and try to save them. As English continues to spread throughout the world and Europe tries to create a unified identity for itself through the creation of a single currency, there is also a growing countermovement to save minor languages. In some regions of Switzerland, Rhaeto-Romance is now taught in schools, and can even be heard on the radio.

Poets are often seen as an important vehicle for protecting these minor languages. You cannot really say that a language is "living" if no poetry is written in it. The fewer number of speakers there are of a given language, the greater the proportion of poets. It is difficult to say whether that is because a dying language tends to convert more speakers into poets, or because the government offers more support for poets writing in those languages. The Sorbian language spoken in the Bautzen district of eastern Germany is a good example of this. There are at most 3,000 Sorbian speakers in the district, although most of them also speak German as well, and I have met three poets who write poetry in Sorbian. Proportionally speaking, that would be like America having 280,000 poets. In East Germany, the Sorbian language received direct support from the government—perhaps because it would reflect well on East Germany if they showed that Slavic minority languages were respected.

The proportion of poets who speak a minor language as their mother tongue is also unexpectedly high, and the same applies to readers of poetry. The German poet Hans Magnus Enzensberger once wrote that on average, a book of poetry sells about 2,000 copies, whether it is published in Croatian or English. The population of the United States is sixty times bigger than that of Croatia. Which tells us that, proportionally speaking, poetry in Croatia sells incredibly well.

However, since few people can read literature written in minor languages, most of the time it ends up getting translated into languages that more people can read. At which point, the vocabulary of the language that is dying out—its rhythms of thought, its way of telling stories, its images and myths—seeks refuge in the major language, becoming dislocated, disoriented, and unsettled. But nothing could be more stimulating to literature than this. Which is why translated literature becomes a vehicle for the transformation of major languages.

When writers who speak a minor language as their mother tongue begin to write in English or another major language, it causes a shift to occur in the major language. And this is not limited to language in the narrow sense of the term. The specific angle from which one regards history, the sensory systems that capture magical things, all of this enters into the language of literature. People from smaller communities have an easier time avoiding the danger of regarding history from the vantage point of the victors. At the same time, magic often manifests itself in minor languages in different ways, due to temporal and qualitative lags stemming from smaller communities' pace of industrialization.

Yang Lian, the Chinese writer based in London, had the opposite stance to Ben Okri's: He had no desire whatsoever to write in English. He said he couldn't stand the kind of flat English used in immigrant literature in England or the United States. Of course, Chinese is not a minor language. When Yang Lian reads aloud in Chinese, the words pour out of him like a torrent. Perhaps it is no coincidence that the next time I saw him was near Niagara Falls. The sheer volume of water was immense. There was something incredibly strong in the current. He told me that one of his favorite poets was Qu Yuan. Later I went back and read "Heavenly Questions" and was fascinated by the rhythm of his thought. How could anyone ever render this in English, I thought. If this is what poetry meant to Yang Lian, I can only imagine how ridiculous it would sound to him for someone to suggest that he write in English. But I think it would be fascinating if the voice of Qu Yuan were to make its way into English and change the current and flow of it from within.

Sofia
Where Words Themselves Reside

THE FIRST TIME I WENT TO SOFIA WAS IN MARCH OF 2000. Everywhere I went, red and white ribbons adorned trees along the road, and the lapels of passersby, signaling the coming of spring. I surrendered myself to the strange, dreamlike atmosphere of the city. In my mind, the faces of pedestrians turned into the Thracians in Tacitus's *Histories*. Europe is full of beautiful old cities like this—Prague and Vienna to name two—but usually, their oldness feels too orderly, artificially tailored to suit the needs of tourists so as not to disrupt modern life. Not so in Sofia, where tourists are quite rare, and daily inconveniences still abound. There is so much to see: Roman ruins, Byzantine churches, Islamic mosques from the Ottoman period, Russian churches, the old art nouveau buildings designed by Vienna-educated architects, Soviet-style structures. You feel the footprints of history everywhere. It is exhausting, but thrilling. Sofia isn't just a tourist attraction where you go to purchase the past in the form of a souvenir. Being there feels like you've fallen into the giant, churning construction site of history.

I often hear German teachers in Japan and the US complain that fewer and fewer students are studying German every year. But this is not true in Eastern Europe, where, at least in some places, the number of German students is on the rise. After the fall of the Soviet Union, there was a dramatic increase in the number of people studying English, but that didn't necessarily mean that people stopped studying German. When I spoke to young readers of German literature in Sofia, they didn't seem to care about arbitrary categories like "east" and "west." If someone liked Chekhov, and so did you, that meant you were friends. This was different from my experience in Germany, where many people perceive an absolute divide between "east" and "west." Whenever I give readings in Germany, I often get the sense that my audience sees Japanese people as aliens from a completely different world.

In Sofia, I got to know the Berlin-based Bulgarian poet Tzveta Sofronieva, who kindly showed me around the city. Although many Bulgarian intellectuals—Tzvetan Todorov and Julia Kristeva, for example—ended up in France, some Bulgarian writers seem to have landed in Germany.

We went to the National Library, where I saw a statue of Saint Cyril and Saint Methodius. I asked Sofronieva whether Bulgaria had adopted the Cyrillic script earlier than Russia. "Obviously," she replied coldly. Thinking about it later, I realized how ignorant my query must have sounded. It would have been like asking a Chinese person if Chinese characters had been used in China before Japan. But Sofronieva didn't write me off. She invited me to Sofia again in the fall of 2002 for a symposium.

Sofronieva had majored in physics and studied abroad in the United States. She started writing poems, and then began to write novels in German after moving to Germany. But she seemed ambivalent about continuing to write in German. She confessed to me that a number of German poets had encouraged her not to.

At the symposium in 2002, a debate took place between several poets from Germany (such as Ulrike Draesner and Brigitte Oleschinski) and a group of Bulgarian poets. The content of the debate doesn't have much to do with the subject of this book, so I'll skip it for now, but what stayed with me was their discussion of Oskar Pastior.

Pastior was a German-language poet from Romania. He was

turning seventy-five that year, so there were a number of events held in his honor. Whenever I read his work, I feel inspired to be bolder in my experiments and take advantage of the fact that I am writing in a foreign language. There's really no point in writing normal novels. In one of Pastior's poems, he takes up the theme of the *heimat* (homeland). But he doesn't fall into the trope of the nostalgic immigrant longing for his homeland. I think he wanted to have a bit of fun with the genre and challenge the expectations around this ideologically loaded term. Historically, the word *heimat* has been problematic for its association with Nazi ideology, similar to the term *sokoku* (homeland) in Japanese. So Pastior decided to put his own spin on the word by dividing it into two parts. Everyone knows that the "heim" in "heimat" means "home" in German, but less attention has been paid to the "at." So he wrote a poem using only words that had that ending, such as "Automat" (vending machine), "Plagiat" (plagiarist), etc. In this way, he simply laughed off the idea of *heimat*, laden with so much history and ideology, by coming up with countless silly words until the whole thing became absurd. Later, I bought a recording of this poem on CD.

The person at the symposium who had been speaking about Pastior discussed how in East Germany, there used to be something called a reverse dictionary, long out of print, that would have come in handy now. Indeed, the whole country of East Germany is now out of print, so there's nothing to be done about that. But it would be interesting to find out why East Germany had printed such a thing at all.

Dictionaries have the power to release words from their ideologies. You might think they exist to arrange words in an orderly fashion, but in fact, they are engines of anarchy. In reverse dictionaries, there are some words with similar meanings that cluster together, and other clusters whose meanings are not related at all. Words whose meanings have nothing to do with each other are drawn together simply because the letters they begin with happen to be proximate to each other in the alphabet.

Thesauruses are the opposite of anarchic, since they intentionally group together words with similar meanings. In German, there are many kinds of thesauruses, but the one I use is the *Dornseiff* lexicon. But I don't like to use thesauruses when I write. When I am in the middle of writing a novel, and need another word to describe a particular scene, it only takes me about two seconds—but those two seconds are incredibly intense, and my brain becomes tired to its very core. If I don't move through those two seconds quickly, the next sentence will escape me. That's why I can't use a thesaurus while I'm writing. But sometimes, maybe on a day where I don't have a deadline looming over me, I enjoy leisurely flipping through the pages of a thesaurus.

The first printing of the *Dornseiff* thesaurus was in 1933, but new editions are still being printed to this day. It is divided into twenty chapters: "Inorganic Matter," "Plants, Animals, and Humans (in the physical sense)," "Space, Length, Shape," "Size, Quantity, Number, Degree," "Existence, Relations, Events," "Time," "Visibility, Light, Color, Sound, Temperature, Weight, Solids, Liquids, Gases, Smell, Taste," "Movement of Places," "Desiring and Acting," "The Five Senses," "Emotion, Feeling, and Personality," "Thought," "Symbols, Communication, Language," "Literature, Learning," "Art," "Social Environment," "Machines, Technology," "Economy," "Law and Morals," "Religion, the Supernatural"—and each chapter has further subheadings. For example, in the chapter titled *Sichtbar* ("Visible") there are subheadings titled "To Appear," "To Form," and a variety of other verbs, nouns like "Outward Appearance," "Visual Field," "Visibility," as well as adjectival verbs like "Standing Out," "Distinguishing," and over seventy-five idioms such as "to catch the eye." One of the stranger sections is called *Ehelosigkeit* ("Celibacy") which lists a variety of colloquial expressions related to the idea of being single. Not only does this include legal terms, but also words like "bluestocking," "virgin," "scion," "misogynist," "soloist," "monk." These are not definitions of words. Instead, they sketch the general movement of a person's chains of thought and association. Looking at this reverse dictionary makes me feels like I am glimpsing the underside of culture.

A thesaurus collects words in the same way someone might collect insects or plants. In fact, while the entry for "Economy" is only fifteen pages long, the section on plants and animals runs at least 150 pages. It may be more accurate to think of this thesaurus as a dictionary of flora and fauna.

Whenever I look at a dictionary, I wonder how words are really arranged inside a human mind. What I do know for sure is that they aren't arranged alphabetically, or according to the Hiragana syllabary. Surely no one hears the word "animation" and immediately thinks of the word *aniyome* (sister-in-law); nor do they hear the word *azukeru* (to lend) and think of *azuki* (red bean). Not only are words not arranged alphabetically in our brains—they probably aren't arranged linearly either. Thesauruses take liberties by changing the order and groupings of words, so they form more of a patchwork. And the inside of our minds is more akin to a surface. In fact, it may be that words are more like 3D objects.

From reading Susumu Nomura's book *Understanding the Brain*, I learned that common nouns are stored in a different part of the brain than proper nouns. That seems intuitively correct to me. I often experience lapses of memory where I cannot remember a proper noun, but it's very rare that I can't recall a common noun. I usually have at least a vague sense of where a common noun is stored in my memory. And if I really can't remember, I can easily reach for a thesaurus and figure it out. But when it comes to proper nouns I often have no recollection of where they are in my brain at all. For example, if I store a proper noun in a drawer of my mind labeled: "Actor's name. Woman. France" then I can probably figure it out pretty easily. But sometimes it feels like that drawer doesn't exist in my mind at all. Some people can remember every actor's name, what movie they starred in, who they're married to or got in a fight with, and other details like that. I suspect that the more vivid the connections are between different names the more likely someone is to remember both. When you store a single name away in a drawer of your mind, it's difficult to find again.

When you're thinking in a foreign language, however, proper nouns and common nouns are often stored together. For example, my eye doctor's name is Dr. Hasenbein (which, directly translated, means something like Dr. Rabbit's Foot). When I think about going to the eye doctor, I find myself searching for the name of my doctor in the "animal" category of my brain. I only go to see him once a year, so his name doesn't come to me immediately. It's the same with my dentist. The other day I was having trouble remembering my dentist's name, when suddenly I realized that I had confused him with my eye doctor and was searching in the "animal" drawer of my brain. But I was looking in the wrong drawer—the one I was looking for was labeled "carpentry tools," since my dentist's name is Dr. Nagle (which translates to "nail").

The book *Understanding the Brain* argues that linguistically speaking our minds do not distinguish between living things and nonliving things, though experts disagree on this. For example, horses and tables might belong to the same memory category because they both have four legs. But maybe this only applies to people immersed in the rich culinary tradition of China, where they say "we eat anything with four legs except the table." Or maybe a memory category like "four-legged" is only relevant in places where Buddhism was influential. The idea of horses and tables being categorized together seems tenable in Japan, but in Germany it would be surrealistic.

In a foreign language, the usual way we categorize words changes, compelling us to think more poetically. For example, German is a foreign language for me, so the words *Zelle* (cell) and *Telefonzelle* (telephone booth) occupy the same place in my memory. This makes sense, since they share an etymology. But for native speakers of German, the word "cell" belongs to the category of biology, while "phone booth" belongs to the category of everyday objects. So in the mind of native German speakers, there's no connection between the two. Perhaps there was when they were children, but as time went on and they became adults, this connection likely disappeared.

People who write poetry often combine words that only non-native speakers would think to mix. For example, the colloquial expression for microwaving something in Japanese is *chin suru* (to "ding" something). Recently I was reading a poem by Toshiko Hirata called "The Power of the Microwave" which tells the story of a character named Chin who goes inside a microwave and is reborn a beautiful being (a Japanese Chin is also a breed of dog). These two meanings of "chin" unexpectedly encounter each other in a place where electrons fly about. And when electrons fly about, it also provokes pleasure in the brain. As the poet brings together words that memory usually stores in separate places and electrons are let loose, perhaps threads like a spider's web begin to grow out of individual words and form connections to new words, constantly overlapping as they move about.

Beijing
Migrating Letters

DURING THE SUMMER OF 2001, THERE WAS A CON-
ference in Beijing for women writers from China and Japan. It was
a gift to be able to meet so many Chinese writers for the first time,
as well as Japanese writers whom I'd previously known through
their work alone. But what I remember most is my encounter
with the Chinese language itself, and the way it changed how I
thought about the relationship between Chinese and Japanese.
It was stimulating for me to think about these two languages
together, since I'd spent so much of my life thinking about the
relationship of Japanese to European languages. Chinese seemed
so close to Japanese and yet so distant at the same time. It was full
of things I didn't understand, and at the same time, things that
felt uncannily close.

After the conference was over, I read a book called *Han Suyin's
Moon* by Yukiko Chino, one of the authors I'd met there. I read it
as a kind of love letter to Chinese as a foreign language. Not since
reading Hideo Levy's *Tiananmen* had I felt such joy at the use of
Chinese characters. The Japanese protagonist's helplessness when
she would encounter a character she couldn't read; the realization
that she actually could read it when she thought she couldn't; the
disappointment of realizing she'd misread a character she thought
she'd understood; the strangeness of how the misreading is what
made the encounter possible at all—the book wasn't just a story
about a young Chinese man and a Japanese woman, but about
what is constantly happening between people, between cultures.

Around the same time the conference was taking place, a collection of writings by modern Japanese women writers was published in Chinese. When a Japanese writer gets translated into Chinese, their name is converted to simplified Chinese characters. I couldn't get used to seeing my name written with the "Yō" in Yoko in its simplified form:

多和田叶子 (*Tawada Yōko*)

I was glad, at least, that the character was 叶 (which means "to be fulfilled or come true") and not 吐 (which means "to vomit"). But I couldn't figure out how the character 葉 had become 叶 in its simplified Chinese version.

I'm sure I'm not the only Japanese person who has a bias against simplified characters. Deep down, many probably feel that simplified characters amount to no more than doodles in the illustrious pages of Chinese history. But when I came back from Beijing and read Toshio Takashima's *Chinese Characters and Japanese People*, I realized that the characters I had grown up learning in Japan were themselves simplified versions of more complicated ones. They had been hastily created at a moment when the Japanese government was considering abolishing Kanji altogether—a tremendous contradiction for anyone who knew the older versions of the characters. As I read on, I began to feel depressed. I'd secretly hoped to escape the world of distorted Katakana loanwords and immerse myself in the beautiful world of Kanji—only to discover that these Kanji were themselves simplified and distorted versions of Chinese. The more I thought about it, the more the Japanese language in which I write and think every day began to seem like some fake thing bought on the black market. It was flimsy (*perapera*) and tattered (*boroboro*)—I suppose this is the only way I can put it if onomatopoeia are the only "real" Japanese words left at the end of the day. If the Kanji system was merely flawed, that would be one thing. No orthographic system is perfect. What made me angry, though, was that these changes to the writing system happened hastily, with the intention of abolishing Kanji altogether. The whole thing seems to have been forced top-down on the population. I wonder if people back then felt like I do now when I can't type a particular Kanji because it's not installed on my computer. You'd think it would be up to the customer to choose what Kanji their computer comes with, but no such luck. It really makes me wonder what kind of people are in charge of deciding what Kanji our computers come with, when I can't even type the character for "ken" in the name Uchida Hyakken.

It's irritating enough knowing that this is the history behind the Kanji I use to write my novels. What's worse, though, is that I don't even know enough to know just how broken and degraded the current Kanji system is. Until recently, I really believed that the Japanese characters I'd grown up learning were the "correct" version, and that simplified Chinese characters were the product of a political failure. As a result, I'd never even tried to learn them, assuming it would be pointless. But when I looked at a Chinese-Japanese dictionary, I discovered that the differences between simplified Chinese characters and Japanese characters could be summed up in two pages. It probably would have taken me less than a month to memorize in junior high or high school. With very little effort, I could have learned a writing system used by a quarter of the world's population. I began to feel resentful of the school I had gone to, which boasted about making its students into "cosmopolitan citizens" while not even bothering to teach us simplified Chinese. But I was partially to blame too. After all, I could just as easily have learned it on my own. The whole thing made me realize how biased my own education had been. It felt hypocritical of me to pity my colleagues who grew up in the former Eastern Bloc, when I had grown up in an education system totally unaware of its prejudices.

Grammatically speaking, Chinese is quite different from Japanese, but because Japanese borrowed the Chinese character system, there is still a certain amount of affinity between the two languages. Linguists used to say that grammar is like the bones of a language, and letters are like its clothing. But nowadays people become friends simply because they have the same shoes, so perhaps bones and clothing are equally important.

I'm inspired in different ways by languages that are more similar to Japanese and more distant. Sometimes when I look at Chinese, I'm overcome by an odd "lag," like I should understand it but I don't. It almost feels like I'm dreaming. At a bookstore in Beijing, I bought myself a small dictionary and learned that the expression in Chinese for being dazzled by something is 眼花繚乱 (yǎn huā liáo luàn) while to faint is 昏過去 (hūn guò qù). It makes sense—to faint means that your past (過去) goes dark (昏). This is already poetry. On a whim I began to write down other interesting words. When my usual vocabulary is broken apart, and reconstituted, something new flickers forth. It feels like a flash in the dark, or a chain that had been wrapped around my brain snapping. Sometimes the joy I feel escapes me in a burst of laughter.

Reading the titles of books by Japanese writers who have been translated into Chinese is itself enough to inspire me sometimes. One of the women writers who organized the conference, Yuko Tsushima, has a work called *Laughing Wolf* (*Warai Okami*) which was translated into Chinese as *Wēi xiào de láng* (微笑的狼). I love this use of the character 的, so different from how it's used in Japanese. Rieko Matsuura's book *Natural Woman* became: 本色女人 (*Běn sè nǚ rén*) or "A Woman of Her Own Character" in Chinese, giving it an extra punch.

When I show people in the US and Europe the Japanese books I've written, they always marvel at the writing system, which makes me feel proud. It's not just because Kanji looks beautiful

and complex. It's also because I know many of them assume globalization has homogenized everything and we don't have anything
unique about our cultures that survives—but here is this writing
system we've been using for thousands of years. Thanks to Chinese
characters, we don't need the West's help in translating concepts
like "communism" or "democracy." Like a castle wall that protects
us from invasion, Kanji preserves the myth of a unique East Asian
culture. Which is why, even though I suffered through countless
Kanji exams in school, I've long gotten over my resentment and
grown to love Kanji with a passion.

Recently I read a book by Akira Yanabu called *How Translated
Words Became What They Were* (*Honyakugo Seiritsu Jijo*), which
describes how the Japanese words for "society," "individual," "modernity," "beauty," "love," "existence," "nature," "rights," "freedom,"
and even pronouns like "him" and "her," were all invented within
the last hundred years in order to translate Western concepts. I
was a bit disappointed to learn this, since it meant that even words
written in Kanji, not just Katakana, were loanwords. In a sense they
were double loanwords, since they originally came from China and
then were used to express Western concepts. At least Katakana is
honest about its foreignness—these Kanji loanwords, though, are
more insidious because they pretend to be original to Japanese.

Though there aren't as many Kanji compounds in novels as there
are in newspapers and articles, I sometimes get the urge to replace
a word like 解説 (*kaisetsu*; commentary) with its variant reading,
ときあかす (*tokiakasu*; to uncover, solve), chuckling to myself in
amusement. Spelled out phonetically, the "toki" in *tokiakasu* could
be 時 (time) or even 鴇 (a crested ibis); while the "akasu" could
mean to grow light (明かす). In this way, it is possible to avoid
Western words and concepts that are simply dressed up in Kanji.

That being said, it's because Japan adopted Kanji that we were
able to translate abstract concepts from the West in the first place.

It also made it easier for us to study Western languages. This makes me a little less angry. For example, while Japanese only had one word for "to look" or "to see" (*miru*), Chinese has many:

見る、観る、視る、診る、看る

Knowing that *miru* contained many different nuances gave me a better understanding of the differences between "to look" and "to see" when studying English. Takashima writes that Japan never really had to develop its own abstract concepts because it existed in such proximity to China, a country that was very culturally advanced. Whether Japan could have developed its own concepts to the same degree had it not had that proximity is an open question. As a pessimist, I'm skeptical. I think it would have been more likely that, similar to Native Americans, our culture would have continued to develop along its own trajectory, and only much later learned English and adapted to Western culture. We would have continued using our own language alongside English and survived modernity as bilinguals, similar to Senegalese people who speak both Wolof and French. Japanese cultural elites who can only speak Japanese would still have access to most things written in Europe and the United States, and wouldn't necessarily have been cut off from information. In fact, there are more translations of German literature into Japanese than there are into English. One can be a member of the international community without being bilingual. In some respects, the ambiguous, impure, and sometimes confusing realm of Kanji, which is neither completely Japanese, Chinese, or Western, may be a saving grace. The realm of Japanese Kanji is an island of dreams. It's also a mountain of trash, but it is rich, and if you sift through it you'll find all sorts of things. You will probably find what you need to survive if you look hard enough. So I have decided to stop being angry and become a resident of the dream island that is the Japanese language, working steadily on like a mouse.

When reading *How Translated Words Became What They Were* I also learned that many Japanese loanwords also came through Dutch translation. When Japanese people set out to translate the word *Schoonheid* (beauty) from Dutch, they considered many options and finally landed on 美 (*bi*). How strange to think that as a child I learned the word for beauty in my mother tongue, and only much later acquired German and learned the word *Schönheit*, only to find that it was the basis of the Japanese word for beauty all along. Which means that many Japanese words I learned as a child were probably words that had "immigrated" into Japanese. Only later when I learned German did I find the real hometowns of these immigrant words. In this way, Kanji is like a costume worn by both Japanese words and neologisms from other languages, which makes them indistinguishable from each other, so that you can't tell where they are from originally. It's strangely moving, then, to realize that many of these words were immigrants who came from lots of different places, and that I've finally arrived at the hometown of the word for beauty.

The word *bi* has an impressive form but a poor physique. Compared to the intellectual and sensual adjectives Sei Shonagon uses in the subtitles of the section headings of *The Pillow Book*—"Things That Make the Heart Beat Fast," "Refined and Elegant Things," "Celebratory Things," "Elegant Sights," "Splendid Things," "Things of Elegant Beauty," "Things Whose Outcome You Long to Know," "Elegantly Intriguing Things"—*bi* just sits there like a lump of concrete. If the concept of *The Pillow Book* is to gather a series of images around each adjective that nestle right up against your nerves, what kind of literature does the word "bi" make possible?

The use of the word *hana*, or "flower" (花) in the *Kadensho* is also interesting. Rather than engaging in endless debate about the beautiful flower or the beauty of the flower, we could have just translated *bi* (美) as *hana* (花). The word "flower" is abstract, yet it has color, fragrance, and a sense of wonder. It is strong but not authoritative, elegant but not pretentious. Perhaps Zeami's vocabulary holds another possibility for translating abstract nouns from Western languages.

The biggest problem with Chinese loanwords in Japanese that are used to translate Western words is that they never really shed their pretentiousness. The reason that *ren'ai* (love) sounds loftier than *irogoto* (sensual pleasures) is not because modern people are finer than people in Chikamatsu's age, but because it was a Western import. Although we no longer think of it as a loanword, the Japanese word *ren'ai* still has a lower body temperature, is more affected and lacking in breadth.

Akira Yanabu, the father of Japanese translation studies, said that the translated word "beauty" has a luxurious aspect to it because, like the outside of a jewelry box, its inner contents remain unknown—and that Mishima managed to make literature seem more lofty by skillfully inlaying it with this word.

In Lévi-Strauss's *Tristes Tropiques*, there is a scene where the chief of the illiterate Nambikwara people imitates a white man by pretending to write, thereby showing his subordinates how great he is. Mishima's use of the word "beauty" is like that.

Which leaves us with the question: How was the Chinese character for beauty (美) created? When I was studying for my entrance exams, I remember reading an explanation—although perhaps it's completely made up—that said something about this character originating among people who lived in the desert regions of China, and that for them, owning sheep was very important (the character for beauty also contains the character for sheep).

So in Germany, whenever I see a big hunk of lamb hanging in the windows of Turkish grocery stores, I think to myself, "Ah, now that's beauty!"

Freiburg
Music and Language

BEGINNING IN 1999, I TOOK PART IN A SERIES OF performances with Aki Takase that involved both music and literature. We performed more than forty times in Germany, Japan, and the United States, but the most memorable—and fun—performance was in Freiburg. Freiburg is an old university town, and it still has that alternative atmosphere of the seventies and eighties, which you can sense from how the pedestrians and cyclists are dressed (there are a lot of bicycles in Freiburg). You feel that especially if you go into a bookstore near the station called Jos Fritz. Bookstores like these were much more common during the student movement, before large chain bookstores took over Germany in the nineties. The smaller bookstores were often run by friends, where there wasn't the typical employer-employee relationship. That ethos lives on in places like Jos Fritz, which is how Takase-san and I were able to perform there.

It's a bit overblown to say that we were dissolving the boundary between literature and music. Plenty of things already do that, including traditional Japanese theater forms like Sarugaku, Noh, Bunraku, or Kabuki, as well as European opera. In fact, you could even argue that for most of history literature and music were inseparable.

In Germany during the 1960s, Günter Grass and Peter Rühmkorf used to perform jazz and poetry sets, but those faded away over time. In northern Germany, there used to be a radio station that had a program called "Kafka: Jazz and Literature," which combined music and literature, but that too disappeared in 1999.

It's not easy to find a venue for such a live performance. It's one thing if the organizer reaches out to the performer directly, but it's almost impossible for performers to find a venue on their own. Readings can be booked at literary centers, libraries, or bookstores; piano recitals can take place at concert halls or jazz bars. But it's much harder to find a space that accommodates both musical and literary performance.

In these kinds of performances, the reading and piano improvisation occur simultaneously. It's more than just a combination of words and music. When I'm reading, the area from my toes up to my throat is completely absorbed in and responding to the music; while the area from my tongue to my brain is pursuing the meaning of the words. Or maybe it's the upper-left part of my body, turned toward the piano, that is responding to the sound, while the upper-right part of my body is sinking into the text. A chasm opens up between the two halves of myself, and it feels wonderful. One part exists outside the world of language altogether, while the other is immersed in it. Of course, they are connected. But they're not perfectly matched—it's more like the relationship between lyrics and melody, an indirect connection, a vibration refracting the air it travels through. If not, my words are just accompanying the music. Or the music is accompanying the words. It's boring when the music becomes part of the background, like an illustration. That's why the music has to be its own, independent thing. Maybe it's because they're independent of each other that a conversation between music and text is possible at all. Sometimes you throw a rock in a lake and wait for the ripples to form, and sometimes what you thought was a lake is actually the back of an alligator, which suddenly rears its head and glares at you. How I read depends on how I react to the music. Of course, sometimes I refuse to react to the music on purpose, letting my own performance shine through.

That too is one way of responding to the music. In any case, there is no manual or textbook—you just have to figure it out yourself. Every moment arises out of countless circumstances, never to be repeated again.

There is music inside of words, but we usually don't notice it. When we read novels, we're too absorbed in the plot or the characters' personalities to notice much of anything else. Take the expression in Japanese *tabetagaru*—to want to eat. When you say the ending of the phrase over and over—"garu garu garu"— you realize it has a very unique sound. The moment that "garu" is separated from the previous part of the verb and becomes its own thing, the sound can no longer be returned to its original meaning. It begins to appeal to something else altogether. As I carry language along with me and enter into this "other language" called music, the strangeness of certain words begins to jump out at me from my own texts. Maybe this is what it means to rediscover language through music.

I've begun to think that the real joy of these performances of words and music lies in each one's repeated discovery of the other's vexing, surplus divisions, their refusal to perfectly match each other no matter how carefully one listens.

Boston

Has English Changed Other Languages?

IN THE FALL OF 2001, I WENT TO BOSTON. IT FELT like a homecoming of sorts, since I had stayed there for a few months back in 1999. This time, I was going to a symposium called "Japan from Elsewhere," organized by Tufts University and Wellesley College. Besides the academics, there were several Japanese American authors there, as well as the poet Hiromi Ito.

This was my first time meeting second- and third-generation Japanese Americans who wrote only in English. I was reminded of how many authors there are with Japanese ancestry who write in English, though I was of course familiar with Kazuo Ishiguro. I also learned that there were academics who write about such authors.

That a writer is an immigrant is not an essential fact in any one literary sense. But sometimes it is useful to think about authors who are immigrants in order to illuminate the migratory nature of literature itself.

In Germany, I've had a lot of opportunities to talk with writers who are second-generation immigrants. When I was a student at the University of Hamburg, I read immigrant literature "classics": Czech writers like Libuše Moníková or Turkish writers like Emine Sevgi Özdamar—in other words, German-language literature written by "anti-German" writers. Discovering their work showed me that it was possible to write literature in a foreign language, even though when I first came to Germany, the idea of writing anything in a language other than my own seemed unthinkable. But after about five years of living there, I wanted to try writing novels in German, too. It was an irrepressible urge—even if someone had told me I couldn't, I wouldn't have been able to stop myself. When you are immersed in a foreign language for several years and are taking in a new language system, part of the theoretical basis for your mother tongue breaks down, changes form, and a new self is born. Some writers strongly dislike this immigrant condition, in which one's "original self" gets broken down. If your mother tongue is Japanese and you've never ventured outside of it, you might hear a word like *yuu suzumi* (evening cool) and feel that it holds some kind of ancient beauty, but once you've stepped outside your mother tongue, you might hear the same word as *yuus zumi* (済み, i.e., used, spent) and suddenly you can no longer believe unconditionally in the coolness of the word. Instead, it appears enlivened, burbling. What is casually beautiful might break along unexpected fracture lines, and may no longer appear natural.

You may be mocked by your fellow countrymen as an unserious punster. But believing in the naturalness of your mother tongue shows a lack of serious engagement with language and belies the entire premise of modern literature. This is why I believe that existing outside of one's mother tongue is not exceptional, but simply an extreme version of the normal state of things.

A couple of days after the conference in Boston ended, I went out to dinner with a few of my German friends who had been living in the US for many years. They asked me what I wanted to eat and I told them I wanted Cambodian food, thinking I'd be difficult on purpose. But they found a Cambodian restaurant right away. I was amazed by how many different kinds of restaurants there are in the US.

At one point in the conversation, they started talking about how their German was getting rusty after living in the US for so many years. Although they saw this as a bad thing, for me it was quite interesting, since it gave me a chance to experience yet another dimension of the German language. Instead of calling the gas station "Tankstelle," they'd call it a *Gas Statione*. Instead of saying "Mir ist kalt" (I'm cold) they would say, "Ich bin kalt," with the pronoun acting as the subject of the sentence, the way it does in English. This made them sound like they were calling themselves a cold, unfriendly person.

One of my friends pointed out that it wasn't just Germans in the United States whose German was changing. Even the German spoken by people in Germany has become more and more like English. The best examples of this are technology-related words, which is also true in Japan. Computer manuals say "Downloaden Sie sich das Programm" (Please download this program). The practice of "Germanizing" a word by adding the -en suffix to an English verb is just the same as adding *suru* (to do) to an English verb to make it Japanese.

It's not as though Germany lags behind the English-speaking world in terms of technology. It played an important role in the history of aircraft technology, yet there is no word in German that corresponds to the Japanese *jisa boke* (jet lag), which forces me to have to use the English word. This strikes me as strange. It's possible the concept of jet lag has nothing to do with aircraft technology. Maybe it was originally thought of as an illness specific to business-men who went on frequent overseas trips, which would explain why only English has a word for it. There's a beautiful German word, *Zeitverschiebung* (time difference), that already exists. The term *Verschiebung* (gap, lag, slippage) strikes me as especially rich because it is the same one Freud uses in *The Interpretation of Dreams*. If only that word could be finessed to create some kind of phrase that meant "the suffering of lag" or "the pain of lag"—but instead, they just imported "jet lag" straight from English. A real shame. It's not that I dislike the English phrase "jet lag," but when it's used in a German sentence it strikes me as rather tasteless. I can't say the Japanese word *jisa boke* (jet lag) is beautiful, but I don't dislike it. The second half of the word, *boke*, means feeling sluggish, "out of it," or senile, and has a certain charm. Perhaps some people are permanently jet-lagged, and can never adjust to existing in this world.

But the influence that English has on other languages is not limited to individual words. At a certain point in time, people in Germany started using the phrase "Das macht Sinn." This is a direct translation of the English phrase "It makes sense," even though originally "Es ist sinnvoll" was the more common usage. Similarly, "Haben Sie schöne Zeit" is a direct translation of "Have a good time!" I still remember an older German teacher telling me not to use that phrase because it wasn't proper German. That was more than twenty years ago, but the fact that she had already picked up on it back then means that people had already begun to use it. Nowadays you hear it all the time, and it's become a completely normal phrase. Something similar has happened in Japan, too. Recently people have started to say "yoi shumatsu o" which means "have a good weekend." When I was a child, I never encountered the word *shumatsu* (weekend) except for when I was reading foreign literature, much less "have a good" something or rather. That was a phrase I'd only see when I was doing my English homework. No one would actually say that in real life. I'm aware I probably sound like a curmudgeonly old person talking about the distant past. But in fact, I'm not that old. When I'm outside Japan, my memories from the "distant past" tend to remain in their original form — so I end up sounding like old Urashima Taro. I imagine that people who have lived in Japan their whole lives, and have seen the language change over time, have hazier memories of this. I relate to my German friends who live in the United States, since they, too, are constantly talking about how much German has changed. In contrast, German people who have lived in Germany their whole lives don't tend to have these conversations as often.

English exists inside German and Japanese. It's not just individual vocabulary words that have been imported, but the general manner of speaking. Which means that even monolingual people are unknowingly speaking multiple tongues.

Tübingen
Translating from a Language You Don't Know

IN NOVEMBER OF 2002, I TAUGHT MY FIRST CREATIVE
writing workshop at the University of Tübingen. I've heard that
in the United States these kinds of courses are quite popular and
also provide an important source of income for authors. In Germany, however, they are rare. Nevertheless, the poet Uwe Kolbe
created a program at the University of Tübingen called the "Studio
for Literature and Theater," where any student can take creative
writing courses in poetry, novels, or plays. I was invited to teach
a three-day workshop there. Teaching someone how to write a
novel is an impossible task, but what I can teach them is how to
become more sensitive to language, shifting the way they look at
it ever so slightly. It is with this goal in mind that I decided to call
my workshop "Translating from a Language You Don't Know."

On the first day, I showed them a single Kanji and had them
write about it. Of course, none of the students had any Kanji reading ability. When I showed them the Kanji for dragon, *ryu* (龍),
everyone paused, and then began writing very studiously. After
an hour, they read aloud what they had written and exchanged
opinions about their work. One student thought it looked like a
blueprint for a kitchen, and wrote a story based on that; another
thought it looked like a festive decoration of some kind, and wrote
a story about a character who feels anxiety on the day before a
big festival; another wrote a story about the frustration of being
unable to read. There was even a student who realized that one
component of the Kanji resembled a pot she'd been looking at

in the classroom, and wrote a poem about how, thousands of years ago, Chinese people had anticipated the pot sitting before her today. Setting out on a voyage to a foreign language without any insurance (read: knowledge) resulted in all kinds of interesting writing. Perhaps stepping outside of their mother tongue released these students from the usual rules constraining their own thoughts—such as that something is too embarrassing to write about.

On the second day, I had the students listen to cassette tapes of different things in Japanese—from sutra chanting to radio dramas. I asked them to choose one recording that they liked and create a translation of it. Some tapes were just recordings of birds or orca whales. Of course there is no way to discern what these animals are saying, so a translation in the conventional sense is impossible. The only thing you can do is follow the sound and write what you hear, or let yourself free-associate and develop something out of that. They all had to find their own ways. If you live in a multicultural society, it's important to think about how you take in a language you don't know, without relying on a dictionary or textbook. I thought this exercise would be an experiment in training them toward that end.

On the third day, we all went to Stuttgart together and wrote on the train ride there. The theme that day was "Landscape as Foreign Language." The landscape visible from the train window must first be "read" by the observer in order to become a text. According to what model do we "read" a landscape? Once we become more aware of that, it can change what we see. Someone who is used to seeing the Swabian countryside will see something different from a tourist who has never seen it before.

Though I am a frequent train traveler, and often write on trains, I have never actually written about the view from my window. Maybe I'm too used to taking the German express and superexpress trains to really notice what's outside. Once, when I was reading Hideo Levy's *Journey to the Last Border*, I came across a vivid description of the inside of a German superexpress train, and the view from the window. It made me realize that people who come from elsewhere often have fresher eyes and see things I don't usually see.

That Sunday morning I was scheduled to give a reading at the Stuttgart Theater. I decided that I wouldn't just read my own work, but also talk a little about the workshop, and then have some of the students read from their work. They seemed nervous to read in front of an audience, but they were well received.

Afterward, an audience member came up to me and talked about how they had recently begun studying Chinese and Japanese at their university, but that they were disappointed because many of the conversational words they were learning were just English loanwords. As a result, they had become bored. I sympathized with them. Here was someone who had taken enormous initiative to learn Japanese, but all they were learning were words like *terebi* (TV), *koppu* (cup), *basu* (bus), *taoru* (towel), *teburu* (table), *doa* (door), *katen* (curtain), *borupen* (ballpoint pen). Anyone would get fed up with that quickly. It was clearly just a list of English loanwords. It would be one thing if learning those kinds of words were easy. The problem is that it's unexpectedly difficult. For example, I once showed a German student who had been studying Japanese for about two years the Katakana word "Rufutohanza" and asked them if they knew what it meant. They had absolutely no idea. Obviously the student was sounding out each syllable in their head, and made no connection to the fact that it was simply a phoneticization of the airline Lufthansa.

By comparison, Chinese seems more fun to learn than Japanese, since most foreign words have to be translated into characters, rather than transliterated phonetically. *Shǒuzhǐ* (which is written with the characters for "hand" and "paper") is much more interesting than the Japanese "toiretto pepa," a mere phoneticization of "toilet paper." Similarly, the Chinese word for TV is *diàn shì jī* (literally, "electronic vision desk"). Compared to that, the Japanese word *terebi* looks lazy and half baked, since it's just the Japanese pronunciation of the English word "television."

In German, the word for television is *Fernseher* (literally something you "see from far away"). So really, Japanese could have done something similar and made a new word using existing Kanji. For example, 遠距離幻 (long-distance illusion) or 電気紙芝居 (electronic theater), 千里眼劇 (clairvoyant theater), or even just 遠見 (distance-seeing). On the train ride home, I decided to make up new Japanese words for everyday objects: *katen*, or curtain, became 目隠し (eye-covering). *Toiretto pepa*, or toilet paper, became しも浄め (nether cleaner). *Borupen*, or ballpoint pen, became 玉筆 (ball pen).

Some Japanese loanwords did get their own Kanji, such as the word for calculator, 電卓 (literally, "electronic table"), or the word for cellphone 携帯 (literally, something that is "carried on the belt"). Some which originally had their own Kanji, like computer 電子頭脳 (literally, "electronic brain") later became phonetic, as computer is now just *konpyuta*.

On days when Katakana is really pissing me off, I try not to use any Katakana words in my writing at all. But then the whole text begins to feel heavy, monotonous, and flat. When I get angry at Kanji and try to write only in Hiragana, the text goes limp and no images come off the page. In the end, I have no choice but to use a mix of Hiragana, Katakana, and Kanji. This is, after all, the history of the Japanese language. But poetry and novels can consciously engage with the flaws of a language in interesting ways—Yoshimasu Gozo's poetry is a good example. Thinking about all of this, I start to feel a little better.

Barcelona
Stage Animals

ABOUT AN HOUR BY TRAIN FROM BARCELONA, THERE is a small, lovely town on the coast of the Mediterranean called Canet de Mar. It is one of multiple places where Lasenkan, an experimental Japanese theater troupe, is based, along with Berlin and Hyogo, Japan, although they perform in cities around the world. It is their multilingual performances that are a special draw for me.

These days, it's not uncommon for people to speak one language in their everyday lives, another at work, and another as their mother tongue. This reality is reflected in Lasenkan's work. In May of 2002 I went to Berlin to see them perform *Sancho Panza*, a play I had written. The performance took place at the Kulturbrauerei, a former brewery with a large courtyard in the middle, as well as a gallery, movie theater, musical instrument shop, literary center, restaurant, and several stages. It still had the atmosphere of an old barn and brewery.

Truthfully, I don't know very much about theater. Still, I have written several plays, or something like them. It's not that I set out to write a play specifically—I just feel that there are parts of every text which want to be translated into voice and movement. Lasenkan understands this—which is why, in addition to being stage animals, they are also, to me, a kind of reading group.

When I'm writing, I sometimes think about how much time people will spend on each word as they read. I want them to read my work more slowly than they would a regular novel, closer to the speed at which they might read a book of poetry. Otherwise, there isn't enough time for the relationship between each of the words to form inside the reader's brain cells.

I have heard that there are some people who do not understand my work when they read it silently to themselves. I assume they are the type to quickly summarize things in their mind as their eyes follow the words on the page. In my texts, a single word might send an image flying off in multiple directions. It takes time for the reader to capture that, then spontaneously create a connection to the next word. Reading quickly won't do. If the word "night" follows the word "dark," then the reader has almost no need to think of a connection between the two; but if there are two words, or sentences, or images, that have no relation to each other, the reader has to create that connection for themselves while they're reading, which takes time. There's no correct interpretation, of course. It's not like solving a riddle. It's a creative act.

More than reading to yourself, listening to someone else read a text aloud allows you to take in more of the content, and the fact that many people experience this proves that speed is a key factor in comprehension. If comprehension is enhanced when one hears a text read aloud, then this is even more true when a text is performed.

It's not just a matter of speed, though—the meaning of a text can emerge differently depending on how it is read (for example, smoothly or haltingly). If a text is intentionally read in a halting way, it can make the text more ambiguous, creating additional possibilities for meaning. If the Japanese word "nokemono" (outcast) is read with a pause after the first syllable: *no / kemono*, for example, it sounds like the word for "beast" (*kemono*).

In Lasenkan's performance, a single sentence would be broken up as it was spoken aloud, not only in German, but in Japanese, Spanish, Italian, and several other languages, becoming distorted and defamiliarized. The actors would repeat the sentence over and over again until it took on weight and, released from its obligation to deliver meaning, entered the realm of music. As I was showered with these fragments of language, I could take my time putting them together and slowly forming my own images. What began to materialize was not "meaning" in the usual sense, but something more three-dimensional—much as our current reality cannot be captured in flat descriptions or definitions, but only as a space where multiple voices crisscross through the air.

For me, the text does not exist to convey a single message. It is more like a structure that continuously shows new sides—and the stage is a place where the necessary time and space can be devoted to that.

In addition to speed control, fragmentation, and repetition, the art of language transformation also uses the difficulties of translation and foreign-language learning to its own advantage. Saburo Shimada from Lasenkan directed the performers Kei Ichikawa, Kana Torino, Angela Nikotola, Jana Ladau, and Maria Nancy Sanchez. Instead of each of the actors speaking in their own languages, the Japanese actors spoke in German and Spanish, and non-Japanese people spoke in Japanese. If each of the actors had only performed in their own languages, the play might have fallen into a sort of Tower of Babel trope, or become a story about people "searching for their roots." But in this performance, each actor had multiple voices. It's not that there are different people and different voices; rather, there are multiple voices inside each person. Which is why the idea of clinging to your ancestral homeland is nothing but an illusion. The only way forward is to create a pluralistic language of im/migrants as we engage with the people who exist together right here, right now.

The use of "accent" in the performance was also interesting. The kind of town a person lived in, the kinds of conversations they had there, and with what kinds of people—all of this is "remembered," or preserved, in their current way of speaking. Just as the kind of German a Japanese person speaks reflects the rhythm of the Japanese language, so too there is a German that is unique to Slavic people, to American people. All of them speak with different accents. No matter how long I've lived in Germany, the past, preserved in my accent, still exists in the way I speak. Of course, Japanese people may have different accents depending on what part of Japan they come from, who they spent time with, etc. The accent is encoded in the memory of the individual. In one scene of the performance, an actor consciously spoke Spanish in a Kyoto accent. In another scene, one of the actors spoke German in the style of a Kabuki actor. These scenes were a reminder that, in the case of im/migrants, the rhythm of their speech does not always correspond to the language they are actually speaking. One German person in the audience later said to me: "There was a point in the performance where I thought the actor was speaking Japanese, and was happily listening along, until I was suddenly disturbed to realize I understood what they were saying: When the hell did I learn Japanese, I thought. But when I listened more closely, I realized they were speaking in German."

Moscow
Who Cares If It Doesn't Sell?

ONCE, AT A SYMPOSIUM HELD AT THE MOSCOW STATE Linguistic University, I read from a text of mine that punned on the Japanese word "kakeru," which can have many different meanings: *megane o kakeru* (to wear glasses); *airon o kakeru* (to iron); *shosetsu no tsuzuki o kakeru* (to be able to continue writing a novel). Later, a Russian scholar and translator of Japanese literature (as well as detective novelist) named Grigori Chkhartishvili came up to me, laughing, and told me that he was going to be in trouble if I kept writing untranslatable things like this. I wanted to tell him that puns aren't just fun—they can also be a powerful ally to literature. But he did have a point: Most of the time, puns are untranslatable. When I thought about it, I realized that it was the texts I wrote in German, more than the texts I wrote in Japanese, that usually contain more untranslatable puns. That's probably because when I write in German, I think from within the language itself, pressing myself up against the words directly.

Of course, it's not always impossible to translate wordplay. There are many different Japanese translations of Shakespeare's plays, but the best are the ones that translate the puns acrobatically. When confronted with an instance of wordplay, a talented translator takes it as an opportunity to display their literary sensibilities.

Which is why translating a literary text brings you up against the limits of language and can be unexpectedly thrilling—not to mention interesting from a literary point of view. Koji Asahina's

Japanese translation of Raymond Queneau's *Exercises de style* is a good example of this.

In *From/Toward World Literature*, Mitsuyoshi Numano remarks that there is no translated text that doesn't have at least one or two mistranslations on each page. And that means, for a three-hundred-page book, a total of five to six hundred mistranslations. I thought it was an astute observation. Anyone who has done even a little bit of translation is vaguely aware of this, but this was the first time I had seen anyone put it so directly. It seems to me that this common notion of "mistranslation" contains within it the possibility of dealing with language beyond the purely moralistic metrics of right and wrong.

Anyone who believes that any text can cross any border and circulate freely simply because we have translators is mistaken. In fact, the majority of texts in the world are either not yet translated or have already been mistranslated. Saying this might imply a rather monotone world, but to me it appears overflowing with color. We cannot travel without carrying the baggage of mistranslation. However, a "mistranslation" and a "correct translation" are not opposites, like a lie and a truth, but are rather both "translatings," journeys—simply different shades of gray. Since every language is different, there is no such thing as a perfectly correct translation. Numano also notes that the presence of a mistranslation does not mean that the entire work is a bad translation. That too is part of what makes translation interesting. Which is why looking for errors in a translation is the easiest task in the world. Even those with only rudimentary experience try to look for mistakes in the work of experienced translators. In some cases, the person who points out an error may be right; but in many cases, what at first appears to be a mistranslation is simply a "detour" that only an experienced translator could have made. Some translators focus on the information the words contain, while others focus on their effect. Still others translate with an emphasis on concept or style. There is a novel by Georges Perec that never uses the letter *e*. Apparently, it is very difficult not to use the *e* in French. There is a German translation of this work, which also does not use the letter *e*. It is also very difficult not to use the letter *e* in German. So this translator's priority was not to use the letter *e*.

One factor that unsettles the idea of "correctness" in a translation is the era in which the work was written. In a Japanese translation, is it more correct for Shakespeare's characters to speak Edo-period Japanese or to talk like high school students from the 2000s? Every time a translator is faced with this kind of decision, they sustain a small injury. Maybe translators are like long-distance runners who bare their wounds as they run. While the runner suffers, the spectator merely points out the wound.

In the original text, there are no "mistranslations." Experimental literature is often compared to a "bad translation," especially in Japan. Perhaps it is precisely when literature has discovered something new that it reveals its "translational" character.

Even "original" works are full of twists and holes akin to mistranslations, and it is these holes that give the work its unsettled quality. So if translation is a necessary evil, then so is literature itself. Or perhaps it is an unnecessary evil. But, as Numano-san writes, "evil" has its own pleasures, sometimes more than "good." And if it is unnecessary, it is even more enjoyable.

That same Numano-san, along with Masahiko Shimada, Amy Yamada, and I, ended up going to Moscow together in March of 2002, where I saw Grigori Chkhartishvili again. We met with a number of contemporary Russian writers, including Vladimir Sorokin, Tatyana Tolstaya, and Victor Pelevin.

In Moscow, I went to an exhibition of Russian avant-garde art where I fell in love with a painting by Alexandra Exter. Colors and shapes jangled together to form an architectural structure, as though the painting were depicting the process of the structure coming together—there was nothing to suggest the depressing weight of a completed building, or the fecklessness of something entirely without form. When I imagine a building in formation, it's not the detailed blueprints of an architect that come to mind, but a scene bathed in moonlight of pipes, boards, and nails dancing around on a construction site after everyone has gone home for the night. It's a captivating painting, and I never tire of looking at it. The catalog also included pictures of the stage set and costumes Exter had in mind. Perhaps for her, the theater was a kind of painting in motion.

When I returned to Hamburg from Moscow, I happened to see another Russian avant-garde exhibit at the Museum of Arts and Crafts. I bought the catalog of the previous exhibit, on Russian avant-garde women, which showed that the transition from avant-garde art to socialist realism was more of a continuum than a break. In a number of cases, I genuinely could not tell which category a work belonged to. I guess this was the point of the exhibit: to wake up a simpleton like me who takes a black-and-white view of history and assumes that the avant-garde is "good" and socialist realism is "bad." After seeing this exhibit, I can no longer look at Natalia Goncharova's folkloric paintings of peasants and static apostles without suspecting that if the angular shoulders were just a little more angular and the slanted chin straightened just a little, it would be indistinguishable from socialist realism. Perhaps the problem lies in the seemingly self-evident nature of each person's ownership over their own bodies. Rather than feel alone in their bodies, they become part of society by participating in agriculture or factory labor. And yet—was it not precisely the moment such bodies had all but disappeared that they emerged as an idealized form? That is why the genre feels strangely hypocritical to me. The government took advantage of people's desire to reclaim this type of body by enforcing a model—whether it served the needs of capitalism or socialism was irrelevant.

But no such body appears in Exter's paintings. Things and people are diffused in an energy spectrum. Her work, simultaneously unsettling and seductive, reflects the total situation of our bodies, words, and space, which can no longer be captured by the trope of "the individual and society."

I don't think this is a problem limited to painting, or even to Russia for that matter. Strangely enough, even Japan, a thoroughly capitalist country, sometimes pushes this trompe l'oeil of "pure-hearted, hardworking people"—and the idea of the "common people" is used to attack so-called experimental art. Yoriko Shono's essays, which criticize the notion of "pure literature," make this quite clear. The mainstream media regularly attacks writers for not "serving their readers" or not "portraying the lives of everyday working people." It would be one thing if they were criticizing the writers for not selling enough books—then it would just be about profit. But instead, they frame writers as "enemies of the people." You would expect that kind of thing in the Soviet Union, but it's strange that it also happens in Japan. In the former Soviet Union, a worker's income was guaranteed, which meant that a writer's income was also guaranteed, as long as they didn't criticize the system. If you were a member of the Writers' Union, the state paid you a monthly salary whether or not you wrote a novel. In the 1980s, there were apartments where only writers were allowed to live, stores where only writers could shop, and so on. In this system, it would make sense for the state to claim that, since workers are the protagonists of the state, the protagonists of the novels must also be workers—and that writers, whose salaries are paid by taxes, must serve the people. It might be a bad policy, but the logic is sound. But this argument makes no sense in a place like Japan, where working people in no way have any kind of guaranteed income and cannot be said to be "protagonists of the state." So I find it extremely annoying that "workers" are conveniently used as rhetorical props only when someone wants to bash the avant-garde. Moreover, since novelists do not subsist on taxes, and are not paid by the state, they are not civil servants and are not obligated to serve anyone in particular. And yet, in Japan, for some reason there seems to be a kind of secret police force in people's minds that forbids any kind of experimentation with prose.

The terms "experimental novel" or "avant-garde" may sound pretentious, but I am not talking about "difficult" literary works. It's simply a question of whether a novel is written with an awareness of language, style, literary history, method, etc. You might even argue that that's the bare minimum when writing anything at all. Of course, this doesn't mean that I am only operating logically when I write. Sometimes I wander into a state of unexplainable euphoria, as new stylistic elements slip into my writing unconsciously. But we must always be aware that the "human" is not a self-evident thing, and that language never pours forth spontaneously from the heart.

Many contemporary Russian novelists, like Sorokin or Pelevin, seem to me to have a clear sense of method. During our round-table discussion, Sorokin declared that he didn't care what readers thought of his work. This is a pretty typical thing for a European writer to declare, but in Japan, writers don't say this kind of thing very often. Amy Yamada responded that she couldn't believe he didn't care about his readers. The discussion ended amicably, but later on, Sorokin admitted that he was happy when his novel was translated into Japanese, since he suddenly became popular with girls there. "So I guess you lied earlier when you said you didn't care about your readers," Yamada retorted immediately. I was impressed by her quick-wittedness, and couldn't help laughing when Sorokin flinched. Later, though, I came to the conclusion that it didn't really matter—after all, it's probably wise for a writer to not assume anything about his readers while he is still writing; and a writer who aspires to write books in order to be popular with girls is a shallow fool.

Moscow has changed a lot since my frequent visits in the 1980s. After the collapse of the Soviet Union, McDonald's and other restaurants opened, and I saw the words "hamburger" and "cheeseburger" written in Cyrillic, which I found amusing. I finally understood why Germans who come to Japan and see the word "hamburger" written in Katakana find it so funny. It made me think the two places were not so different after all. When I see words like "credit" and "bank" written in Cyrillic, I feel a little bad—it's like being shown something out of a dream, a Russia that's been tainted by capitalism. I have no particular feelings about Germany, but I have a sentimental attachment to Russia. However, that kind of sentimentalism is ultimately empty, not too different from Japanophiles who feel sad that the beautiful version of Asia they had constructed in their imaginations doesn't exist. Rather than become a "Russophile," I'd rather visit and read more about the Russia that exists today.

Marseille
Toward the Horizon, Where Words Dissolve

I WENT TO MARSEILLE FOR TEN DAYS IN THE SUMMER of 1999 on a sister-cities artist exchange program: Each year, two to three artists from Marseille go to Hamburg and vice versa to read and translate each other's work with the help of an interpreter. Joachim Helfer, a writer who came to Marseille with me, could speak French, but none of the writers in Marseille could speak German.

With the help of interpreters, we all worked together every day from morning to night huddled in a room in the library. Part of me wondered whether ten days wasn't too much—I thought two or three might have been sufficient. But the organizer, a young woman who seemed quite passionate about her work, said it would be meaningless if the program were too short, so I surrendered myself to whatever plans she had.

In hindsight I am very glad I participated, as I got a lot out of the experience. It was there that I met Bernard Banoun, who later translated two of my books into French. Listening to a language I didn't understand every day allowed me to experience a special state of mind I had never experienced before. I was paired with a young writer named Véronique Vassiliou, and speaking to her through an interpreter—listening to what she said, and then listening to the interpreter translate what I'd said to her—meant that I was listening to French for four hours a day, every day. I expected that would be a waste of time, since I don't speak or understand French, but during the conversation it felt like my whole body had transformed into a giant ear. I couldn't not listen, nor did I feel that listening was a waste of time. Instead, the sounds of the words, the gestures, body heat, and light made me feel strangely fulfilled. Everything was there except for the meaning of the words. And when night fell, something unusual would happen. I'd have the strangest dreams—some of the strangest I've ever had in my life, almost as though I'd been drugged.

In my dream, a brightly colored snake slithered languidly across the ground, and tree buds glistened in the sunlight. The green of the buds leapt over the boundary separating me, the observer, from the image being looked at, and began to extend inside of me. Moreover, it was absolutely clear to me in the dream that the snake and the buds were language itself. But that didn't mean it was abstract. In my dream, this "language" was raw, so close to my body that it didn't seem possible for it to be any closer. My emotions lost their armor and garments and stood there completely naked. The slightest tremor in the air made me want to cry, scream, even kill. I had a premonition that if things continued this way, something terrible would happen. All distinction was lost between words and things, and my nerves were completely exposed. Is this the kind of world I'd secretly been seeking? It was terrifying, and at the same time, I had never experienced life so vividly. Perhaps at its core, language is merely a potent drug.

The day after the workshop ended, I gave a reading at a small theater in Marseille. The plan was for all of us to fly to Hamburg the following day to do a reading at the French Cultural Center. I spent the entire taxi ride into Hamburg talking with Joachim Helfer. The excitement of the workshop had not yet cooled. I was so engrossed in the conversation that I'd lost track of time, until I suddenly realized that the cabdriver was going down a strange road. It ought to have been a straight shot from the airport to the venue, but now he was turning right and left at every block,

winding through residential areas at incredible speed. When I
looked closely, I glimpsed a few buildings that seemed familiar,
and we seemed to be going in the right direction overall. Why was
the driver going to all this trouble when he could have just taken
the main road? I saw him gritting his teeth. I realized then that
he was angry—here we were on our high horses, talking about
literary theory, completely ignoring him. This wasn't the first time
I'd experienced this. Most Japanese cabdrivers are professionals,
but many German cabdrivers are former teachers, poets, or artists
struggling to make ends meet. This driver probably heard us chatting away about literature to each other, arrogantly assuming he
was just a driver who wouldn't understand our conversation. But
this town was his language, Hamburg's roads a grammar only he
understood. He continued weaving through the streets like a rat
running through a maze, cutting corners as he raced on. I began
to feel nauseated. I suddenly wanted to cry. I had finally made it
home, only for this to happen. Was this just a continuation of
losing myself in French?

I realized later that I have never listened to a language I didn't
understand for as long as I did then. Thanks to this experience,
French has come to occupy a position of "pure language" in my
mind. Some might argue that if I'm going to spend so many hours
listening to a language I don't know, I may as well study it. But
there's something priceless about that state of unknowingness.
I'm sure eventually I will study it, but I want to savor this suspended state of unknowingness for a while. How much creative
stimulation can we draw from the state of not understanding at
all or from the state of still understanding only a little? When I
was first learning German, I was so desperate to learn it quickly
that I never had time to actually notice this. But I think at this
point in my life, I can simply observe myself stumbling and falling
without feeling too much shame about it, surrendering myself to

the state of being unable to communicate. Once people are able to communicate, they do it all the time, without thinking. That's all well and good of course, but language also has a mysterious power within it. Maybe what I am really searching for is a language that has been freed of meaning altogether. Perhaps the reason why I ventured outside of my mother tongue to begin with, and why I keep seeking a world where multiple cultures overlap, is because I am searching for that state just before individual languages are dismantled—freed from their meanings and finally annihilated.

II
Adventures in German

Caretakers of Space

ONCE, WHEN I WAS STUDYING AT THE UNIVERSITY of Hamburg, I heard about an interesting lecture that was coming up, so I called an acquaintance and asked which "Zimmer" it would be held in. I heard them chuckle on the other end of the line. They ended up telling me where the lecture was, but for the longest time I couldn't figure out why they had laughed. Eventually I learned that a university classroom is not called a "Zimmer," but a "Klassenzimmer." To refer to it as just a "Zimmer" is incorrect, although one could have called it a "Raum."

I learned all this not because I looked it up in a dictionary but because, years later, I suddenly remembered this conversation and realized that *Zimmer* does indeed conjure up a warm, private atmosphere, perhaps carpeted, with furniture—a far cry from the hushed public space of the classroom. I had learned the meaning of the word through conversations I'd had over the years, until finally it had settled in my mind as an image.

On the other hand, it would be perfectly reasonable to refer to a living room or a bedroom as a "Raum." At a basic level, any space is a *Raum*. Its meaning is quite broad. It can also refer to the abstract idea of space, as in *Zeit und Raum* (time and space). The interesting thing about German is that the same words used in everyday speech are also used in philosophy books, making it easier to connect everyday situations to abstract ideas.

Take the profession *Raumpflegerin* (literally, cleaner of space), also known as a *Putzfrau* (cleaning lady). In one sense, the cold, abstract nature of *Raum* makes the word seem more dehumanizing. On the other hand, maybe it's an attempt to scrub away the grime of discrimination that's historically been attached to the profession, by using a more objective term to describe the work of cleaning. *Raumpflegerin* can be translated as "caretaker of space" or even "nurse of space," implying that a dirty or messy space is a sick space. As this example shows, a poor literal translation can sometimes have a poetic effect. It was the poet Ginka Steinwachs who once added a *t* to the beginning of *Raumpflegerin*, thus changing it to *Traumpflegerin* ("caretaker of dreams").

When you reserve a seat on the German superexpress train known as ICE, you have a choice between sitting in the *Grossraum* (the regular car) or in an *Abteil* (compartment). The word "Raum" is so ubiquitous in everyday speech—the changing room you use before you get in the pool is the *Umkleidraum*, for example—that you barely notice it. Still, it never really loses its abstract quality. A storage room is an *Abstellraum*, and sometimes an *Abstellkammer*. *Kammer* sounds darker and dustier than *Zimmer*, at least in my mind, though I'm sure there are nondusty ones too. Then again this may be disrespectful to *Kammermusik* (chamber music). It would be more precise to say that *Kammer* simply refers to a small, narrow space.

Then there's *Spielraum*, another very common word that means having "leeway," as in when you leave yourself ample time, rather than making plans at the last minute. It draws attention to the way every action needs a certain amount of time and space. The word *Spielen* (to play) also has a broad range of meanings. The ability of everyday words to cover such a wide array of meanings is almost dizzying.

One of my favorite words is *Zwischenraum*, the space between things. It's difficult to translate into Japanese, because the word *kuukan* (space) already contains the meaning of "betweenness."

At a recent cultural festival in the town of Schwalenberg, there was a panel discussion about a project where a dozen poets would pick a spot in nature and write a poem about it. A Swiss architect named Peter Zumthor built a small structure at each site and placed the poet's poem inside of it. Visitors would then stroll through the fields and forests between the villages, reading the poems as they went. The project grew out of the idea that books may not be the only space in which poetry can live. Could a structure built outdoors also become a *Raum* for poetry?

There were several things I found interesting in this discussion. A musician named Walter Fendrich said that space shouldn't be thought of as a "container" to hold objects, but as something that is created by the presence of objects themselves. When a single note of music is played, it doesn't occupy some space that preceded it, but creates the space through its emergence. Similarly, when a thought comes into your mind, it creates a new space in the world. It's not a matter of first creating a container and then filling it; rather, when you create a word, it brings a space into being. I wish I could get this idea across to those who are all too eager to build museums, concert halls, and literary centers, but remain indifferent to what is inside of them, thinking that they have created culture simply by building a container for it.

Trifling Words

WORDS HAVE THE POWER TO HURT, ANGER, OR RE-
assure. There is a small word in German called "nur" (only). In
Japanese, this is usually translated as *shika* or *tada* or *dake*. By
themselves, these may not seem like words that can have such an
impact on people's feelings. But I have offended people with this
word on numerous occasions.

I still remember one time—after I had given an interview at the
Norddeutscher Rundfunk—when I asked the young woman who
was in charge of cultural programming at the time: "Arbeiten Sie
nur für den NDR?" (Do you only work for the NDR?) She replied
angrily: "Wieso? Das reicht doch!" (What's wrong with that? It
seems fine to me!)

I was at a loss for how to respond. Recently many German
radio stations had to cut their staffs due to financial difficulties,
and more and more people were working freelance for multiple
broadcasters. Which is why I wanted to know what other TV or
radio stations might be hosting her literary programs. However,
she seemed to take offense at the question.

Later, when I told this story to Ms. B., a native German speaker,
she told me that it wasn't the word "nur" that was the problem—
this employee was simply neurotic.

However, it was not until much later, when I spoke with the
poet Thomas Kling, that I realized I should use the word "nur"
with some caution. Being a poet, he is quite sensitive to language,
and if he doesn't like someone's attitude or something they say, he
will point it out straightaway. If I'm remembering right, I think
we were at a coffee shop in Graz at the time, talking about theater.

I was telling him that most of the time, Noh and Kabuki actors only (here I employed *nur*) use classical Japanese, and that, for this reason, when having them perform in a German play, it would be necessary to translate it into the appropriate sort of Japanese, rather than the modern standard kind. He quickly pointed out that it would be more appropriate to use the word "ausschliesslich" in this context. I thought about it and realized he was right.

Of course, the distinction between *nur* and *ausschliesslich* is not so strict in colloquial speech, but it is better to use the latter in cases where it might be interpreted as derogatory or accusatory. The Japanese words "shika" and "dake" are somewhat similar in this regard. If you say, *Ano hito wa doitsu bungaku dake o yatteiru* (That person studies only German literature), the implication is that German literature is the person's specialty, so that's what they spend most of their time studying. But if you say, *Ano hito wa doitsu bungaku shika yatteinai* (That person only studies German litera-ture), it implies that he or she should be doing other things as well.

The word "ausschliesslich" is not only quite harsh, but also a bit cold. Perhaps it's because the verb "ausschliesslichen" liter-ally means to shut something out that I'm not very fond of it. For example, the fact that I only do literature and not music or painting is because I simply lack the time and ability to do them all. To express this, I would say *Ich schreibe nur* (I only write). In response, people might say "What do you mean, 'only'? Being a writer is no small thing!" Still, I feel *nur* captures my feelings best.

Similar to the word "aussliesslich" there is also the word "ledig-lich." I like this word even less. It may seem that I am obsessed with talking about my personal likes and dislikes of individual words, but I think this is actually an important part of learning a language. It is better not to use words you don't like. After all, this isn't a school cafeteria—it would dull our sensitivity to language if we adopted the motto "eat all your vegetables." If you dislike a word, there is always some reason for it, even if you cannot explain it immediately, and it is usually tied to your personal memories and aesthetics. So while letting loose with my personal proclivities and antipathies toward particular words, I'd also like to explain the reasoning behind my choices.

The reason I don't like the word "lediglich" is because people often use it when they say things like "I am just doing my job" or "I am just asserting my rights." Isn't the phrase "I'm just doing my job" merely an excuse that police use when they arrest protesters and are criticized for it afterward? When I think of this word I think of a face that is asocial, emotionless, tired, inflexible—a face like a bureaucratic document.

The word "nur" on the other hand is small and cute. It focuses its attention on one point and shines a spotlight on it. *Ich möchte nur Dich einladen* (I wanted to invite only you over). *Bei mir gibt es nur Gutes zu essen* (There's nothing but good stuff to eat at my place). Sometimes, limitations increase the value of something.

The word "nur" can also have the effect of reassuring people. *Nur zu!* (Go ahead!) *Nur nicht ängstlich!* (No need to be afraid!) These phrases are designed to reassure or encourage someone. In that sense, it's similar to the word "einfach," which means "easily" or "simply" and can also be used to reassure people. For example, say someone wants to go to the university office to ask about enrollment procedures, but they don't yet have an application form, or a residence permit. Perhaps they don't know whether they need to go to another office first. They don't have money, they haven't found a part-time job, they don't speak German well, etc., and they're worried about all these things. In addition, there's a high chance that the employee working in the university office will not be very pleasant to deal with. To someone who finds themselves in this position we might say, *Du kannst einfach hingehen und fragen, ob … ?* (Why don't you just go and ask … ?)

In this way, small words can anger people or reassure them, and this is simultaneously strange, fun, and dangerous.

Lying Words

THIS YEAR, I WAS ONCE AGAIN ASKED TO BE A MEM-
ber of the jury for a literary award in the German state of
Baden-Württemberg. The theme was: *Wenn die Katze ein Pferd
wäre, könnte man durch die Bäume reiten* (If cats were horses, humans could ride through trees). In one sense it's odd to have a
theme attached to a literary award. But the fact that people submit
manuscripts based on a particular theme also made it interesting.
Of course, since it's not a college admissions essay, it is completely
up to the author whether they want to ignore the theme completely, deal with it indirectly, or address it directly in their work.

The sheer diversity of responses to this "proverb" or theme
amazed me. Some of the characters in the stories would say things
like "Cats are not horses, so this prompt is too silly to even think
about" or "I am not interested in fairy tales." In German there's a
saying: *Erzählt mir nur keine Märchen* (Don't talk fairy tales). In
Japan, too, *otogi banashi* (fairy tale) is sometimes used with some
disdain to mean an unrealistic story.

The Japanese language also has the word "esoragoto," literally
"empty pictures," meaning a "fabrication" or "pipe dream," which
carries a disdainful attitude toward something that is unrealistic.
I find it annoying that paintings are used as a metaphor for lying.
If someone says that's nothing more than an "esoragoto," I might
reply "Does that mean photographs are more accurate?"

Lumping together words like "make-believe," "fabrication,"
"fiction," "bullshit," and so on, implies that making up stories is a
bad thing. But it would be a disaster if fiction disappeared. Fiction

is also a useful framework for capturing things, and we would lose our sense of direction in life if it were to disappear.

When I go into bookstores in the US, the books are often separated into "fiction" and "nonfiction." Perhaps this is a practical division that is easy for customers to understand. Things are different in Germany, however, where the word "Fiktion" refers to fiction in a more abstract sense, rather than a literary genre. That makes much more sense to me. Even autobiographies and history books are, strictly speaking, fictional, since the author collects, interprets, selects, fills in the blanks, and reassembles the material according to their own view of history. I believe that even a diary is a kind of fiction. Fiction is not about lying, but about using language to construct a building.

In Germany, what is called "fiction" and "nonfiction" in the US are more often divided into the genres of *Literatur* (literature) and *Sachbücher* (practical guides, manuals, or how-to books).

Are there any examples of musical genres being used as a metaphor for falseness? No one would ever say, "He's just playing a fugue," to refer to someone who lies and evades responsibility, or "They're just conducting a string quartet," to refer to people who aren't telling the truth. German idioms sometimes mention the fiddle, but it has nothing to do with lying. When we speak of "playing first fiddle," we mean that someone occupies a leadership role; while one who "plays second fiddle" takes less of a visible role in things. In German if someone says *jemandem grünlich die Wahrheit geigen* (literally, "playing the truth on a violin") what they mean is not that someone is lying, but that they are telling the absolute truth to the very marrow. Should we literary types be jealous that music is never considered untruthful? Perhaps music is so different from reality that it cannot be compared. And maybe literature and paintings can lie because they seem to reflect reality, but do not.

As I write this, though, I am remembering that there is a Japanese phrase, *hora o fuku*, which literally means "to blow a trumpet." Apparently music, too, can lie.

Theater lies by its very nature. The German phrase *Theater machen* (to do theater) means when a person complains in an exaggerated way in order to demonstrate a point rather than to express their true feelings. In Japan, too, people sometimes say *shibai suru* (literally, "to do theater") or *shibai gakatteiru* (to be theatrical). The phrase *mie o kiru* (to strike a pose) also comes from theater.

There is a particularly strong aversion in northern Germany to disguising one's true feelings. The metaphor of the "mask" is often used to convey the idea of hiding behind a lie to cover up one's real feelings. Incidentally, there is also the Japanese phrase: *Noh men no yo* (like a Noh mask). However, that such an expression exists in Japan always struck me as strange. Do people really think that Noh masks are expressionless? For me, there is nothing more expressive than Noh masks. A phrase I find more interesting is *neko o kaburu* (literally, "to play the cat") which means "to be a hypocrite."

The antipathy to acting in everyday life is much stronger in Germany than in Japan. Many Germans talk about how they find store employees in the US and Japan unpleasant because you can't tell whether they are being sincere. In Hamburg, where I live, many shopkeepers are quite brusque. It's not that they're unkind, but that they don't believe in smiling just because a customer happens to be buying something. If you are in a bad mood on a particular day, they believe it's better to be honest about that. However, since I grew up in Japan and assume that all shopkeepers are friendly, I feel annoyed when German ones are brusque. But then I go to Japan, see the "elevator girls," and immediately feel homesick for Hamburg. In Japan, the ideal employee always smiles even when they have to respond to unpleasant customers—this is common practice. How would a Japanese shopkeeper respond if asked whether they were being theatrical? They would probably say: "It's my job."

Hands, Feet, and Other Organs Hidden Inside My Vocabulary

I WAS ONCE INVITED TO UNIVERSITY COLLEGE DUB-
lin to give a workshop in German. The professor who invited me
wanted the workshop to be based on a concept that comes up in
one of my novels, which I call the "flea market."

In my novel *Ein Gast* (The guest), the main character passes by
a flea market and begins to make all sorts of associations about
fleas. The term "flea market" is so commonplace that we don't
usually think of the actual insect when we use it, but doing so can
yield some interesting results. When I think of the word "flea,"
the German idiom *jemandem einen Floh ins Ohr setzen* comes to
mind. Translated literally, it means "to put a flea in someone's ear,"
but what it actually means is to put someone on to an idea. The
person to whom the idea has been suggested is restless, can't stop
thinking about it. Imagine how unsettling it must feel to have an
insect inside your body.

Although not a "flea" specifically, the Japanese word "mushi"
(bug, insect) can also refer to one's subconscious. Rather than
someone planting an idea in you that you can't get rid of, this
"insect" is something that exists inside of you from the beginning,
influencing your thoughts and ideas, ignoring reason and seemingly acting of its own accord. The phrase *mushi no idokoro ga warui*
(the bug is in the wrong place) means to be in a bad mood. The
idea is that if this bug is not in the right place, it will easily become
irritated by the most trivial things. Similarly, *mushi ga sukanai* (the
bug dislikes it) means you simply don't like something or someone

for reasons you can't explain. *Mushi no shirase* (a premonition from the bug) means you have a bad feeling about something, and *hara no mushi ga osamaranai* (the bug in your stomach won't calm down) means you can't contain your anger about something.

There are lots of interesting images hidden inside words and idioms that we normally don't think about at all. The aim of this workshop was to do exactly that. It's also easier to notice these things when you are learning a foreign language than when you are speaking your mother tongue. I think this is because our mind categorizes words in a foreign language according to a different logic than in our mother tongue. They're stored in an entirely different chest of drawers. For example, for a person whose mother tongue is Japanese, the expressions *mushi no idokoro ga warui* and *kigen ga warui* belong to the same drawer in our minds because they both mean "to be in a bad mood." For those whose mother tongue is not Japanese, however, the word *suzumushi* (bell cricket) may be closely linked to *mushiba* (cavity) and *yowamushi* (coward, wimp) because they all have the word "mushi" in them. Idioms in your native tongue are like meals—you simply eat them the way they're served to you. But in a foreign language, you are more apt to notice how the idiom is formed. It appears more raw, like a side dish you might be tempted to add your own ingredients to.

A Nabokov scholar once told me that Nabokov changed the English expression "to cut a long story short" to "to cut a long story quite short." In Japanese, you could do something similar: The phrase *temijika na* (brief) literally means "short-handed," so you could easily change it to *ashimijika na* or "short-footed."

The intention of this workshop was to look at language from the outside and let that stimulate us in a literary way, taking advantage of not being a native speaker by refusing to eat ready-made dishes.

There were workshops which included Irish teachers and students of German. The teachers actively participated and seemed to enjoy themselves. In the first one, we looked at phrases like "flea market," which, despite their commonplace status, bring up a host of interesting images upon closer inspection.

The first German word the students came up with was *Faulpelz*, meaning lazy, but whose literal translation is "rotten fur." The same student suggested *Frühstück*, meaning breakfast, or, literally, "early piece." That student wrote a story about a man who wakes up in the morning with his body covered in rotten fur, walks to the kitchen dragging it behind him, and forces himself to eat his breakfast piece by piece (*Stück für Stück*) even though he doesn't want to eat it. It was a story that resonated with anyone who has a hard time getting up in the morning.

Another participant, a high school teacher, came up with several words and phrases that included the names of animals. *Katzentisch* (the "kids' table" but literally the "cats' table"); *Affentheater* (a "charade" but literally "ape theater"); *Hundewetter* ("very bad weather," literally, "dog weather"). Someone else brought up words that include names of flowers. Dandelion is a *Löwenzahn* (literally, "lion's teeth"). A pansy is a *Stiefmütterchen* ("stepmother"). Perhaps this is why flowers, which are supposed to be beautiful, sometimes appear to bare their teeth at me like something out of a horror movie.

Finally, we gathered all the words and made a list. Then, each participant picked out one or more that they found interesting, that felt inviting or tickled their intellect in some way, and then wrote a short sentence based on it. If we separate the word "Atemzug" (breath) into its component parts, we get *Atem* (breath) and *Zug* (train). So, someone wrote a story about traveling on their own *Atemzug* (breath) as though it were a train.

In the second workshop, we identified names of German cities that included names of body parts, and then each person chose one city name and wrote a sentence about it. For example, the city of Dortmund includes the word *Mund* (mouth). Darmstadt includes

Darm (intestine). Although not very famous, in the northwest of Hamburg there is a town called Itzehoe (*Zeh* means "toe"), which one person wrote a fictional tourist commentary about. According to the fictitious pamphlet, the town is divided into ten districts, five on each side of the river in a fan shape. The northernmost two districts were larger, the southern two smaller, and the other six were about the same size. The paving stones in the streets of each district were bright red in the summer. Other place-names included Saarbrücken (*Rücken* means "back"), Maulbronn (*Maul* means "mouth"), Potsdam (*Po* means "bottom"), Garmisch-Partenkirchen (*Arm* = Arm), Rehmagen (*Magen* means "stomach"). We even got into a discussion about districts within cities, such as Kreuzberg in Berlin (*Kreuz* means "waist"), and Haar in Munich (*Haar* means "hair").

Play can temporarily free us from the habit of seeing words solely as tools for conveying meaning, allowing us to come in contact with the language itself. Through touch, we learn the cultural history inscribed in the body of language, and visit the illusory city of the heart. During the Edo period, Japan had a thriving culture of *Kakekotoba*, or wordplay. In fact, it's always been an important part of Japanese literature. Wordplay may not be as common in Germany, perhaps due to Prussian seriousness. But precisely for that reason, I would like for people to think of German as a language they can play with.

On Mistranslating the Moon

THE OTHER DAY, A JAPANESE FRIEND OF MINE WHO lives in Germany read a German translation of Matsuo Basho's *Narrow Road to the Interior* and asked if I hadn't found the translation a bit "off." When Japanese people criticize translations of Japanese texts, they often insinuate that the translator didn't really understand the text. I think this is because, somewhere deep down, they believe that only Japanese people can understand the real meaning behind works of classical Japanese literature—even though if they spent any time abroad with foreign scholars of Japanese literature, I'm quite sure their prejudice would disappear.

In any case, my friend had commented on the opening line of *Narrow Road to the Interior*, arguing that the German translation of *tsukihi wa* was incorrect. I didn't recall feeling that the translation was wrong when I read it, so I went back and looked at this part of the text again. The line was:

月日は百代の過客にして

Tsukihi wa hakutai no kakaku ni shite
(Days and months are the travelers of eternity)

The translator had rendered the phrase *tsukihi* as "Sonne und Mond" (sun and moon) in German. My friend argued that the translator had made a novice mistake in rendering *tsukihi* as "sun and moon" when it actually meant "time" in classical Japanese. They said it would be like someone translating the Japanese word *mujun* ("contradiction") not as *Widerspruch* but as *Hellebarde und Schild* (spear and shield), since that is what the characters mean at a literal level.

And yet, I found this particular German translation of *Narrow Road to the Interior* quite beautiful. When I thought about why, I came up with the following explanation: When medieval people used the phrase *tsukihi*, perhaps they used it to refer to time not in a metaphorical sense, but in a literal sense, so that the phrase evoked the rising and setting of actual suns and moons. They must have had a completely different relationship to time compared to a modern person like me, who simply glances at the neon digits glowing in the corner of her computer screen and thinks, "Today is May 18," or, "Gosh, it's already 10:00." It's not that the sun and the moon no longer exist in the modern era, but that we don't use them to tell time anymore—so they've become metaphors for time, rather than real markers of it. In this sense, translations that are so literal as to border on being mistranslations sometimes force us to look at the origins of a word, rescuing us from the senility of its mere metaphorical form.

I think the use of *tsukihi* in the opening line of *Narrow Road to the Interior* is beautiful, as is the use of *Sonne und Mond* in the opening line of its German translation. The word "time" would have felt too abstract here. For me, *Sonne und Mond* conjures up a concrete image of the moon as a traveler outside my window, a temporary visitor who will return home in the morning. I was quite moved by this, as I had never thought of the moon as a traveler before.

A similar example: The phrase *ugetsu* in the Edo-period work *Ugetsu Monogatari* ("Tales of Moonlight and Rain") is translated literally into German as *Regenmond* (rain-moon), as that is what the characters in Japanese literally mean. I remember a student of mine who was majoring in Japanese once asked me whether the translator hadn't made a mistake and meant to write *Regenmonat* (rain-month) instead, since the words for "month" and "moon" are the same in Japanese. In that moment I realized, much to my embarrassment, that I had never really considered what the word *ugetsu* meant. Did it refer to the fifth month of the lunar calendar? Or did it mean the moon on a rainy night? Would the moon actually be visible on a rainy night? Was the phrase supposed to conjure up an image of the moon's light reflecting off the rain—or was that just my own interpretation?

When I looked at the German translator's afterword, it turned out that they had intended the word "Regenmond" to mean the fifth month of the lunar calendar. In other words, they had intentionally translated it that way. The word "Regenmond" (rain-moon) doesn't exist in German. If the translator had used *Regenmonat* (rain-month)—a perfectly normal word in German—it would simply have conveyed the idea of a "rainy season" without invoking any imagery or feeling. It makes me think of Southeast Asian travel guidebooks that will often warn you not to travel during the *Regenmonat* (rainy season). *Regenmond* (rain-moon) on the other hand, whose meaning I can't quite place, is more alluring, and better conveys the mood and atmosphere of the stories in *Ugetsu Monogatari*. Perhaps we can say, then, that the "mistranslation" pointed out by the student was actually the correct one.

Surely every translator has had the experience of inventing their own word when they can't find the right one for something they are trying to translate. If I can be forgiven for referencing my own work, I once wrote a poem in Japanese called "Tsuki no Toso" ("Flight of the Moon") which included the following line:

月のような不安、月のような憂いも消えて

Tsuki no yo na fuan, tsuki no yo na urei mo kiete
(An uneasiness like the moon, a sorrow like the moon
has disappeared)

The German translator Peter Pörtner translated this as: *Die mondgestaltige Angst, der mondgestaltige Kummer sind weg* (Moon-shaped fear, moon-shaped sorrow has gone away). He had made up the adjective "moon-shaped." I specifically didn't want my moon to be a metaphor for anything—I wanted to invoke the actual moon here, since the poem told the story of a moon that escapes on a bicycle.

In a poem called "Wunder der Liebe" ("The Miracle of Love") by Ludwig Tieck, there is a line that includes *Mondbeglänzte Zaubernacht* (a moon-glittering, magical night). A bit romantic for my taste, but it's one that's always stuck with me, as the moon is often invoked in poems from the Romantic period.

When I first came to Germany, I remember thinking that the word "mondsüchtig" was quite interesting. Translated literally, it means "moon-addicted," but the actual meaning is more like "sleepwalking." A coworker of mine told me that it refers to someone who is lured outside by the moon while they are still asleep. I was a little freaked out by this, wondering if maybe German moons had the ability to hypnotize people. A drug addict is referred to as "drogensüchtig," an alcoholic as "alkoholsüchtig," so it's interesting that a somnambulist is referred to as a "mondsüchtig" (moon-addict). In my German-Japanese dictionary, I found the word *tsukiyohokobyo*, which literally translated means "moon-wandering-sickness." Sometimes I come across Japanese words in my German-Japanese dictionary that I haven't encountered anywhere else, which stir up new images and bring me great joy.

When you want to describe someone who is a bit behind the times, you can use the phrase *Er wohnt hinter dem Mond* (He lives on the other side of the moon). For example, I have an acquaintance who is a philosopher and lives in a basement buried under a mountain of books. He's managed to successfully avoid modern society for the past forty years. A couple of years ago, he came over to my friend's house and was surprised to see that she had a color TV, rather than a black-and-white one. Whenever I meet people like this I'm tempted to invent a new word in Japanese to describe them: *tsukiurajin*, a "behind-the-moon person."

Pulling Stories

DRAWING A LINE FROM ONE POINT TO ANOTHER CAN be a fun activity. In some children's magazines, there are "connect-the-dots" drawings where a fairy tale landscape emerges once you've drawn in all the lines. Sometimes you can even color the picture in, which makes the "plane" created by the lines stand out more clearly.

Over the course of spending a long time with someone, you begin to see different aspects of their personality. One of my favorite German words is *Charakterzüge* (characteristics), which is made up of the words for "character" (*Charakter*) and "lines" (*Züge*). So I decided to make up an equivalent word in Japanese: *seikakusen* ("character lines"). You know that a person has a temperamental personality when you see them fly into a rage not once, but twice. The first and second incidents are points, and when a line is drawn between them, their personality becomes visible to you.

But humans are more complex than this, and lines are not always easy to draw. Maybe the first time you meet someone they open up to you, but the second time they're unexpectedly cold. And as you collect these contradictory pieces of information, a number of lines begin to emerge. As more and more lines appear, the "surface plane" of a personality begins to take shape. But this can be tricky. Sometimes you look closely at what appears to be a line, only for it to disappear in a flash in the next instant, so that the plane never fully solidifies.

A word that's related to *Charakterzüge* is *Gesichtszüge* (features, expression), made up of the words "face" (*Gesicht*) and "lines" (*Züge*). A facial expression is something fleeting. Maybe it's not that the expression "appears" but that our eye is able to perceive extremely subtle movements that pass as quickly as the flight of a bird. The face of the person we think we are seeing may actually be something much more formless, whose shape never quite settles into something definite. The expression itself makes the "face," rather than any static, predefined features such as their "big eyes" or "long nose." But if facial expressions are dynamic, then the gaze of the person perceiving them must also be dynamic. Just as predators have a keen eye for things that move, but not for things that don't move, so human beings must have evolved to perceive elements in the face that run or run past. These are just some things that come to mind when I think about the word "Zug."

Of course, "Zug" can mean "train" in addition to "line." A railroad draws a line from one town to another. In Japanese, the word "densha" or "ressha" (train) has nothing to do with a "line," but *senro* (railroad) which is made up of the characters for "line" and "road" does.

The word "Zug" is also closely related to the verb *ziehen* (to pull), since the first train car "pulls" the rest of the cars behind it. *Ziehen* is a fairly commonplace verb. We wake up in the morning and put on clothes (*sich anziehen*). Our clothing (*Anzug*) might consist of work clothes (*Arbeiteranzug*), sports clothes (*Sportanzug*), or swimwear (*Schwimmanzug, Badeanzug*).

Many people drink black tea in the morning—the act of "steeping" the tea, bringing the flavor out of the tea leaves, is *ziehen lassen*. In Japanese, this is *umami o hikidasu*, literally "drawing out the umami." We don't say that we "draw out the tea" (*ocha o hikidasu*) but rather "the tea comes out" (*ocha ga deru*). Though I'm not sure whether the tea comes out because the hot water draws it out, or whether the tea enters the hot water on its own.

To return to the breakfast scene, we also have *natto* (fermented soybeans), at least on the tables of people who prefer Japanese-style breakfasts. *Natto* is notoriously stringy (*ito o hiiteiru*, literally "it draws string"). Other kinds of food in Japan also have this quality: yams and okra, for example. Some people believe that this "stringiness" is good for one's health.

In Germany, if you want to check how much money you have in your bank account, you can go and get a *Kontoauszug* (bank statement). This will list all the money you've withdrawn and deposited, as well as your current balance. The phrase *okane o hikidasu*, to withdraw money, also uses the verb *hiku* (to pull).

Raising children (*großziehen*) is also a type of *ziehen*. Raising a child is *Erziehung*. When a child turns eighteen, they often become independent and move out (*ausziehen*) of their parents' house. That moving residences (*Umzug*) is also a type of *ziehen* prompts me to consider the Japanese word for moving (*hikkoshi*). Sure enough, it, too, includes the character for "pulling." At first, it's common for people to rent an apartment, or live with their friends. Later, they might get into a relationship (*Beziehung*). But then they might break up or get into a new relationship, and each time that happens, they might have to move (*Umzug*) again, until finally they get so fed up that they just retire (*sich zurückziehen*).

Come nighttime, most people cover their mattress with a sheet (*Bettbezug*), their pillows with a pillowcase (*Kissenbezug*), and go to sleep. Here again, we find the hidden *Zug*.

A phrase I often hear is *Es zieht*. In Germany, when a draft blows through a room or a train, people will frown and say, *Es zieht*, then quickly close the windows. Drafts are bad for your health. Just as falling asleep in front of a fan can be dangerous, drafts take body heat away from the skin. But that's not the only reason people fear drafts. There is a superstition that bad spirits passing through a house may cause misfortune. After living in such a cold country for many years, I gradually came to understand the horror of feeling a draft blow through an interior.

The most charming example of a word that involves the con-. cept of "pulling" is *Anziehungskraft* (allure, magnetism). Literally, it is the ability to "pull in people's attention." Sometimes we see someone and our eyes and ears are immediately drawn to them, and our feet move toward them involuntarily. Perhaps we live in a state of constant motion, pulled along by invisible threads.

Spelling Words

THE LITERAL MEANING OF THE JAPANESE WORD
sakubun (composition)—which is written with the characters
for "to make" and "text"—is really quite blunt. The image that
comes to mind when you think about "making" something is
of gathering materials, using tools, putting things together. But
writing isn't at all like that. As you write, something invisible flows
out of the surface of your skin and language begins to move like
a living creature. Your body temperature may become slightly
elevated, and you may enter into a slightly euphoric state as you
abandon your ego altogether. This process does not at all match
the craftsmanlike feeling of the word *tsukuru* (to make). I wondered if there wasn't another word that more accurately described
the act of writing, something that captured its magical quality.

The German word *Aufsatz* is equally dry and sobering as the
Japanese *sakubun*. It describes an essay you might write in school,
or a scholarly dissertation. When a clearer distinction is desired,
the former might be called a *Schulaufsatz* (school essay) and the
latter a *wissenschaftlicher Aufsatz* (scholarly essay). Often these
aren't long enough to be proper books. Instead they might be
included in a collection of essays.

The word *Satz* ("sentence") comes from the verb *setzen*, which
means to put something firmly in its proper place and to feel it
settle, in other words, to "set." So *setzen* is used when the right
sentence is put in the right place, when an article of clothing fits
perfectly, or when an actor says a line just right.

There is also the word *entsetzen* as in *Ich war entsetzt* ("I was appalled"). The prefix *ent-* implies distance from something. Perhaps this is because when we encounter something unexpected and terrible, we become appalled, and the shackles of reason, common sense, and emotion fly off, leaving us hanging in midair.

The verb form of *Aufsatz* is *aufsetzen* (to set something on something else). But unlike the noun, the verb cannot be used in the context of writing an essay. Instead it's used to describe a variety of everyday activities, such as putting a kettle or pot on the stove, putting on a hat, putting on glasses, and so on.

It would be funny to imagine setting our thoughts over a flame, warming them up, bringing them to a boil, and simmering them down. In the process they might become overcooked, soggy, or lose their flavor.

Although a bit old-fashioned, there is another, related Japanese word, *tsuzurikata*, which means writing or spelling. This could refer to stringing words together to make a sentence, but it also calls to mind weaving. The character looks like this:

綴

The left side of the character is the radical for "thread" while the right side is the radical for "again" repeated four times. I think it is looks like a beautiful, ornate brocade. In modern Japanese, the word *tsuzuri* only refers to writing in the most narrowest possible sense—that is, spelling. But I prefer the original sense of the word, which included the idea of writing itself, which is much broader than "making."

In 1999, I was invited to be a writer-in-residence at MIT in Boston for about four months. During my time there, I taught a German class and asked my students to write a few essays. In addition to the three longer essays I had them write over the semester, I also asked them to write two short essays per week describing their thoughts on the previous class, their thoughts on the novel they were reading in preparation for the next class, etc. Then they would submit this essay before each class.

Since MIT is an engineering college, most of the students were majoring in math, science, or technology. They were only taking German because the liberal arts program required them to take a foreign language and literature credit, so it's not as though any of them were aspiring writers, or even literature majors. They didn't read novels regularly or keep a diary. Unexpectedly—or maybe for that very reason—some of the students seemed to enjoy these writing exercises and the "essays" they submitted each week got longer and longer. Their essays weren't limited to talking about the books we covered in class. Sometimes they would veer off topic and start talking about a fight they'd had with their girlfriend that day. One student said that although he didn't usually write, he enjoyed it once he started. It was interesting to see a group of students who didn't normally write in their mother tongue begin expressing their feelings, dreams, and even personal matters in a foreign language, all because of an assignment in a language class.

If you are studying a foreign language, I highly recommend keeping a diary. You might make grammar or spelling mistakes, but try not to worry too much about that and just enjoy writing as much as possible. You may find that you're able to write freely about things that you might feel too embarrassed to write about in your mother tongue. As you do this every day, your sentences cumulatively begin to weave a new self, rather like a textile. To learn a foreign language is to create a new self, to discover a self that is unknown to you.

In Japan, we become adults, learn about the world and how to interact with people through the medium of the Japanese language. And it is Japanese that has shaped what we are and aren't allowed to think about or say. So as long as I'm writing in Japanese, the impulse to avoid certain taboo subjects is automatically activated. When I write in other languages, however, this function goes dormant. I find myself being bolder and expressing things I would never have thought to say otherwise. Memories from my childhood that I had long forgotten about suddenly come flooding back to me.

Before she died, the Czech-born German-language writer Libuše Moníková said that she could not have written one of the most important parts of her novel, in which a character is subjected to violence, if she'd written it in her mother tongue. It was writing it in German that proved to be her literary breakthrough.

Some experts argue that psychoanalysis only works in one's mother tongue, but perhaps someday that won't be true. It seems plausible that some things are actually easier to talk about in a foreign language. Why not write in German about the most embarrassing thing you have ever done, or the person you hate most?

BodyBody

A SWISS FRIEND OF MINE WHO LIVED IN JAPAN FOR a few years recently told me they loved the word *karada* (body). The direct translation of the word in German is *Körper* but the two words have completely different meanings. For example, in Japanese it's common to say "*O karada o kiotsukete*" (literally "Take care of your body") when you want to wish someone well, but in German you would never tell someone to take care of their *Körper*. That would sound very strange indeed. It would be the equivalent of telling someone to take care of their flesh. The German word *Körper* calls to mind something that interferes with a person's spiritual or intellectual activities—like sexual desire or physical appetite—so the more accurate Japanese equivalent might be *nikutai* (flesh).

In a modern context, the phrase *Karada ni kiotsukete kudasai* means something more like "Take care of your health." But again, if you translate this into German directly—*Achten Sie auf Ihre Gesundheit*—it sounds very strange. Perhaps you might say this if the person was gravely ill, but in an otherwise normal context, your interlocutor might begin to worry that they look excessively pale.

Some say that *karada* comes from *kara*, which means empty, because the body is an empty vessel. But plenty of people in other countries share that view of the body too. They believe that if the body is an empty vessel, is well managed and healthy, then it won't get in the way of spiritual activities. At the same time, if the body is just an empty vessel, then nothing can come out of it either. The saying "A sound body implies a sound mind" also makes it seem as though the body is a mere container for the mind.

On the other hand, the idea of the *Körper* as having inherent value, separate from the mind, has recently gained traction. For example, I am right-handed but whenever I press a button I do so with my left hand. This is a habit from a period of time in my childhood when I broke a bone in my right hand and couldn't use it, so this memory lives in my hand. It may be that the body remembers things that the mind has forgotten, and that the body can express itself in its own language. This suggests that the *Körper* is not mere baggage, but one center of human life. It has even become a bit of a buzzword. Of course, there is also something sinister about this way of thinking. Lately, it has even become common for meditation clubs and new religions to advertise their "health" teachings by claiming things like "You are living too much in your head. You need to unify your mind and body."

However, the revival of the *Körper* as something honorable also suggests the plurality of the human subject, which has become a key idea in literary studies, especially in the past twenty years. Say you want to go to school, but when you actually try to go, you get a fever. You both want to go and don't want to go—both are true at the same time.

What excites me most is the idea that not only human beings but also languages have bodies. In Japanese, for example, *buntai* (literally, the "body of the text") means "style." It's as though a sentence not only conveys a certain meaning, but also has a body of its own, with its own temperature, posture, illness, habits, and personality. In other words, language has a living body and cannot be reduced to semantic content alone. I often think of the words *Klangkörper* (literally, "sound body") which means ensemble or orchestra, and *Schriftkörper* ("body of writing") in relation to language. Language not only conveys meaning, but also has its own echo, and that echo has its own meaning. The same can be said of letters. In calligraphy, it's obvious that the shape of the script is part of the meaning, and this is true of regular handwriting as well. The letters of the alphabet make it possible for me to write the things I want to write, and at the same time, they snatch the ideas away from me, incorporate them into their own bodies, so that the sentences I write become independent of me. A friend once told me that they didn't like writing because when they wrote, they felt like their feelings were becoming separate from them, that they no longer belonged to them, and once they set their feelings down on paper, their content seemed to change from how they'd actually experienced them. Which is why they preferred to keep their feelings to themselves and not write anything at all. Such people should definitely not become writers. After all, the act of writing entails keeping company with language, which has a body separate from the author's own.

If *Sprachkörper* is the body that belongs to language, then *Körpersprache* would be the language of the body. This isn't language comprised of words, but of gestures, a kind of communication through the body. This is useful when traveling to a foreign country, where you don't speak the language. However, gestural language also differs from culture to culture. For example, one time a friend of mine went to a Japanese person's house. She had to walk down a long, narrow hallway to get to the bathroom, and accidentally passed it without realizing. The Japanese host beckoned to her to get her to turn around. To my German friend, however, that gesture, a kind of waving with the palm facing down, means "go the other way." So my friend kept walking further down the hallway, while the Japanese host repeated the same gesture again and again, growing increasingly desperate.

If you put a *Maneki-neko* (a "beckoning cat") in a store in Germany, it's possible that it will have the opposite effect as it does in Japan, and keep both money and customers away.

In Germany, the gesture of rubbing the tips of your index finger and thumb together means "money." Tapping the forehead with the index finger means that the way someone is doing things is "off." This action alone will undoubtedly get your meaning across, but it is often accompanied by the idiom *Er hat einen Vogel* ("He has a bird [in his head]").

It is often said that Italians use more gestures than Germans when speaking, but of course there is a great deal of variation across individuals. When people become impassioned as they speak, I notice that they often rotate their right hand outward. The force of the rotation sometimes increases when they are emphasizing a word or phrase, so listeners should be careful not to get in their way. As far as I have seen, it is always an outward rotation of the hand, never an inward rotation. Once, when I was at the University of Hamburg, I videotaped an academic seminar and a few of us watched it together later. We had a good laugh noticing the excessive amount of "body words" the speakers used which usually escape our notice.

Garments

BECAUSE CLOTHING IS EXTERNAL TO THE BODY, WE usually don't think it has a direct connection to human emotions. When you are sad, your forehead may wrinkle, but your blouse won't crease. Conversely, just because you are in a good mood doesn't mean that your unpolished leather shoes will shine.

However, there are many idiomatic expressions that suggest that people's feelings may indeed seep into their clothes. Take the German word for necktie (*Schlips*), for example, or the expression *jemandem auf den Schlips treten* (literally "to step on someone's tie"), which means "to insult someone." You might think a necktie is just a piece of cloth that hangs around your neck, but imagine someone stepping on it—it may be that, unbeknownst to you, your self-esteem has actually seeped into that flimsy piece of cloth. Even though I've never worn a necktie myself, it's an expression I can relate to on a physical level.

There are several expressions in Japanese that pertain to this idea of wounding someone's pride or feelings: *Hito no kimochi o fuminijiru* literally means "trampling on someone's feelings." Similarly, *dosoku de hito no ie ni fumikomu* (literally, "entering someone's house with your shoes on") means inserting yourself in other people's business. Since the necktie is something that came from the West, there are no Japanese idioms that have to do with them, or with pockets. We do have sayings that use *futokoro*, the breast pocket inside a kimono, even though most people no longer wear them on a daily basis. For example, there's the saying *futokoro ga atatakai* (literally, "to have a warm breast pocket") which means to be flush with cash. It may be that idiomatic phrases outlive the fashion that they originated in. For example, considering how old the word *mago* (packhorse) is, it's surprising that we still use the phrase *Mago nimo iso* (literally, "There are clothes even for a packhorse"), meaning anyone can look good with the right clothes.

While hats are no longer worn very often, they still show up surprisingly often in idioms, such as when people say "*Hut ab!*" ("Hats off!") to show their respect to someone. *Ihm ging der Hut hoch* (The hat flew off of him) is another phrase you still hear frequently. It means that someone got so angry that they lost their cool. If neckties are associated with pride, then it seems hats are associated with anger.

A hat has a unique shape. Magnified, it looks something like an architectural dome. Domes are places where people congregate. When a group or organization has many different personalities, perspectives, and opinions, the Germans say *unter einen Hut bringen* (literally "to bring people under one hat") which means to bring people together.

Shrink the hat, and you get *Fingerhut*. This is a cap-shaped thimble made of metal or ceramic, which is placed over the finger when sewing. It is a curious little object. Some people might buy it as a souvenir when visiting Austria or Germany.

The collar seems to be associated with justice. In movies people often grab someone by the collar and shake them while angrily questioning them. The phrase *jemanden beim Kragen nehmen* (literally "to grab someone by the collar") means "to question someone" and perfectly describes this scenario.

In Japanese, *eri o tadashite* (literally "to straighten your collar") means to shape up or straighten up. It seems to imply that if you straighten your collar, your mindset will be straightened up as well. This tells us that the collar is associated with seriousness. Therefore, if you want to live carelessly, you can just wear a collarless T-shirt so you never have to straighten your collar or worry about being responsible for it.

In German, if you tell someone to tighten their belt (*den Gürtel enger schnallen*) you are saying that they should suppress their extravagant desires and save money. The belt, figuratively speaking, divides the human body into upper and lower components. The upper part is the head and face, the public part of the body governed by reason, and the lower part is more personal, involved with digestion, excretion, sexual intercourse, etc. I myself do not agree with such a dichotomization of the body, but that seems to be the way many people think. The border separating the two worlds is *die Gürtellinie* ("the beltline"). So when a joke or a snide remark ventures into the sexual realm, it is said to have gone "below the belt" (*unter der Gürtellinie*). I always felt this idiom was quite vivid. It's strange how the word "belt" seems more explicit than waist, navel, or stomach.

Unlike a belt, an obi is soft even when tightened. To "loosen the obi" means to let down one's guard and relax. However, this is no longer a very common expression in Japan today.

Sode no shita (literally, "beneath the sleeve") means to "bribe someone." Where exactly the bribe is hidden in the sleeve is hard to say. Politicians may sneak wads of cash into their sleeves, while magicians pull pigeons and rabbits out of them. There is a German saying, *aus dem Ärmel schütteln* (literally, "to shake something out of your sleeve"), which means to pull something off with ease.

Finally, *in die Hose gehen* (literally "to go into the trousers") is when something has gone terribly wrong. I have no idea why this is the case. The image I have is of someone putting a gold coin in their pocket, which then falls through a hole in their pants.

When I first moved to Germany, I was impressed by the phrase *tote Hose* (literally "dead pants"). Say you go out at night, perhaps around ten o'clock, in a small town. All the bars and restaurants are closed, there are no dance clubs or movie theaters, no one is out, and you're feeling bored. People will say, "After ten o'clock, it's *tote Hose* there." I don't know why pants come into play here, and I always wondered why the pants are "dead" when they aren't even alive to begin with. If you ever go to a small town in Germany and find yourself with nothing to do at night, I urge you to remember the phrase *tote Hose.*

Sensed Meaning

THE JAPANESE WORD KANNO, MEANING "THE SENSES" or "sensuality," is strange when you look at it closely. The character for *kan* is the same character used in the word *keisatsukan* (policeman) while the character *no* is the same that's used in *noritsu* (efficiency). Both profoundly unsexy words. But combined, they mean "sensual," even though separately they are associated with having a certain function, being in charge of something, or having the power to do something. When I imagine the sensory organs being aware of their respective roles and working hard to do their job, I realize that being "sensual" must be a very difficult job.

I was in for another surprise when looking into the German word *sinnlich*, which means "sensual" and is derived from the noun *Sinn* (sense, meaning). However, the word *sinnvoll*, with which it shares a root, has a completely different meaning of "purposeful," "rational," or "meaningful." For example, someone might tell you to reserve a seat on the train today because tomorrow is a holiday, or that you should buy travel insurance when going abroad because regular health insurance won't cover it. All of these actions would be *sinnvoll*. If I mistakenly said that it would be *sinnlich* (sensual) to reserve a seat on the train, the listener would have to use a great deal of imagination to understand what I meant.

The Japanese word *kannoteki* is much less common than *sinnlich*. Unfortunately that is part of the reason why the concept of *Sinnlichkeit* has become so commodified. In cosmetics or tourist ads, you might see a person in a bathing suit, the sun shining down on her, drops of seawater glistening on her skin, head tilted back, eyes closed, lips slightly open. This is *Sinnlichkeit* in a nutshell. If you ask someone who lives a gray corporate life if they want to spend some *sinnlich* time together, they will no doubt jump at the opportunity.

Although *sinnlich* refers to physical pleasures, it is not always overtly sexual. It hints at the sexual while pursuing the pleasures of sunbathing or the gastronomical delights of the tongue. But in Japan, I rarely see advertisements that show bathing or eating in a sexual light. You never see ads of tongues touching sashimi, or beautiful young men bathing in hot springs and gazing at their own skin in rapture. In Japan, bathing and eating tend to be portrayed as cool and refreshing, rather than hot and sensual.

The opposite of *sinnvoll* is *sinnlos*, which means "useless." For example, a person who does not have a regular job and continually writes novels that nobody reads may be told by family and friends that there is no point in doing that (i.e., it is *sinnlos*) and that it would be much better for them to get a real job. But for this person, writing may be a *sinnlich* experience that gives him a truly sensual pleasure. Then again, a girl who falls in love with a playboy who is sexually attractive but has no job or money may find that skipping school together is *sinnlich*, but her parents and teachers would never say that it is *sinnvoll*. Perhaps they would call it *sinnlos* or even worse, *Unsinn* (absurd) or even *Blödsinn*, which means the same thing but is harsher in its denunciation and more colloquial (something like "bullshit").

When you think about it, many *sinnlich* actions are considered by society at large to be *sinnlos*.

For many religions, *Sinngenuss* and *Sinnlust* (pleasures of the flesh) are not only *sinnlos*, but also *Sünde* (sins). But in today's society, some have figured out how to tame pleasure so that it doesn't interfere with economic life, but rather encourages it.

When people say that something is meaningful or not meaningful, it sounds logical enough. But in the end, *Sinnesorgane* (the "organs of sense") are what really determine whether or not something is meaningful. There's the saying *sinnerfülltes Leben* (a "meaningful life") but I'm always tempted to ask which version of *Sinn* is meant here. A meaningful life sounds admirable, but you can still be left with a feeling of emptiness even if you are doing admirable things. There really is no objective standard, and in any case, the senses must be part of the equation.

Meaning (*Sinn*) isn't determined through common sense. It is captured by one's own senses (*Sinn*). The sense organs are the basis of meaning. For example, if you eat something and it tastes good, you won't feel that it was a waste of time. If you climb a mountain and enjoy the view, or listen to music you like, then you will not feel that life is meaningless. Perhaps it is when the senses are not capturing something delicious that we begin to search for meaning. But that doesn't mean that the more luxurious your consumer life is, the better. It often happens that someone goes to a gourmet restaurant and doesn't like the food.

In the end, it's the person who is able to enjoy bad food who wins. In order for something to taste good, one may have to study literature and many other things. It is not the animal tongue that decides whether something tastes good or not, but the message that the taste buds carry to the brain, where it passes through a web of many things, including the person's ideas, experiences, and moods.

Although I just used the word "animal," I am in no way discriminating against animals here. Even my cat, who looks disgusted when I give her cheap canned food, will gulp it down if I put a spoonful in her mouth. To put it in literary terms, descriptions that are only *sinnvoll* but not *sinnlich* are problematic. No matter how meaningful it may be for the reader, a sentence that merely explains why the protagonist is going to his aunt's house is useless if the words are not pleasurable to read. One might say that *sinnvoll* is transmission and *sinnlich* is expression. Some people might think that the pleasure of language is only for poetry, but this isn't true at all. Novels must also be pleasurable to read, otherwise they fall short.

Translator's note

ALTHOUGH YOKO TAWADA IS A BILINGUAL WRITER, *Exophony* is clearly addressed to a Japanese readership. In many ways the book is about the Japanese language itself, and is Tawada's own reckoning with her native tongue, after so many years of living in Germany as a kind of exile. But as she writes in the introduction, "exophony," the condition of existing outside one's mother tongue, can also illuminate much that isn't visible to a monoglot. Here, as always, to write for Tawada is to innovate: "Fish that I am, I used my scales to feel out the linguistic textures of each place as I went swim-walking about." In Japanese, she uses *arukioyoida*, a portmanteau of her own invention that combines the words for "to walk" and "to swim." It is as though Tawada's immersion in German, a language so rich in compound words, has given her the freedom to rewrite the rules of Japanese—and of reality. Here is Tawada the cheerful loner, the amphibian, the more than—or other than—human.

The ocean metaphor is significant, too. While nation-states may artificially impose borders on parcels of land through brute force and rally their populations around a single tongue, identity, and national mythology, Tawada understands that language, like water, often exceeds the rigid (and violent) borders imposed by states. In *Exophony*, she is alive to that fluidity in so many details: She notices the eleven different languages in which the news is broadcast on South African TV; the way her encounter with Chinese refracts her own native Japanese back to her as in a "dream"; and all the minor languages kept alive in rural regions of Switzerland.

When she does reference German words, Tawada takes care to

explain their meaning to her Japanese-language readers. Translating this book into English, then, meant that I needed to do for my English readers what Tawada had done for her Japanese ones by providing in turn occasional glosses and explanations for Japanese words (since Tawada did not have anglophone readers in mind when writing this book). Still, without a basic framework of the Japanese language, *Exophony* can at moments prove challenging to navigate, and, so, a brief primer for the uninitiated:

Unlike most languages, Japanese uses three different writing systems: Hiragana, Katakana, and Kanji. The historical reasons for this are complex, but suffice to say that Kanji ("Chinese characters") are directly borrowed from Chinese and often share a semantic meaning with their original counterparts. However, they are generally pronounced differently in Japanese than they are in Chinese, similar to how the Spanish word "manifestación" and the English word "manifestation" look similar on the page but sound different when spoken aloud. Kanji are also logographs, meaning that they have a semantic component as well as a phonetic one (unlike letters in an alphabet, which only represent sounds and have no inherent meanings). At the same time, Japanese also uses two syllabaries—Hiragana and Katakana. Like alphabets, syllabaries represent only sounds, not meanings. Hiragana is used to spell out words native to Japanese, while Katakana is used to spell out "loanwords" (i.e., words not native to Japanese).

These distinctions become important in "Seoul," when Tawada laments the overuse of Katakana loanwords in Japanese as a symptom of hypercapitalist globalization. For her, nowhere is this more apparent than in the language of ads, where every other word is Katakana:

おしゃれな大人の女性をターゲットにした、
ライフスタイルのトータルブランドとして先
シーズン、デビューし、二回目のコレクショ

ンとなる今回は、新しくオープンした丸の内
のショップでコレクションを開催。

Not only is this visually striking on the page, but the effect in
Japanese is of a sentence almost totally devoid of meaning, littered
with English loanwords as pure instruments of marketing. Since
English does not have a second alphabet I could use to mimic the
effect of Tawada's Katakana words of consumerism, I hope the
small caps here recreate the sense of empty excitement induced
by these vague words:

> The latest SEASON of our TOTAL LIFESTYLE
> BRAND series DEBUTS its second COLLECTION at
> our newly OPENED Marunouchi location PERFECT
> for stylish young women!

Elsewhere in the book, Tawada is critical of the way English—and
Western culture generally—continues to function as a vehicle of
aspiration and desire for Japanese people who don't dwell on the
past or on the power dynamics between different languages.

The differences between Hiragana, Katakana, and Kanji are
also important to understanding a chapter like "Barcelona," where
Tawada plays with the possibilities inherent in Kanji compounds
to invent another Japanese portmanteau: *idomin* (移動民). In
reality, no such word exists in the Japanese language. Rather, it
is a combination of the words *ido* (移動, movement, migration,
or travel) and *imin* (移民, immigrant). Unlike an *imin*, then, an
idomin suggests not someone who moves from point A to point B,
but someone who is simply on the move, in motion. To capture
her linguistic playfulness here, I have translated this in English as
"im/migrant," to suggest a person in a state of perpetual transit.

Tawada's questioning of borders—not only between nation
states, but also between languages—leads her to question the

boundaries between music and words, voice and text, human and animal, even words and things. In "Marseille," she writes: "In my dream, a brightly colored snake slithered languidly across the ground, and tree buds glistened in the sunlight. The green of the buds leapt over the boundary separating me, the observer, from the image being looked at, and began to extend inside of me... it was absolutely clear to me that the snake and the buds were language itself." Tawada's dream calls to mind Jack Spicer's words in *After Lorca*: "I would like to make poems out of real objects. The lemon to be a lemon that the reader could cut or squeeze or taste—a real lemon like a newspaper in a collage is a real newspaper. I would like the moon in my poems to be a real moon...a moon utterly independent of images. I would like to point to the real, disclose it, to make a poem that has no sound in it but the pointing of a finger."

Like Spicer, Tawada longs to dissolve language altogether, understanding that the point is to undo its artifice rather than cling to it. A firmly antinostalgic writer, she rejects the concept of a homeland, a mother tongue, or any sort of attachment to a national identity. For her, linguistic dislocation is not something to be mourned but celebrated, as it allows her to recognize the artifice inherent in any language, freeing it up as an instrument of play. "Maybe what I am really searching for," she writes, "is a language that has been freed of meaning altogether." Of course, as she acknowledges in "Seoul," her ability to experience exophony as a state of freedom rather than its opposite hangs on the fact that as a Japanese person she has never experienced colonization: "People have no right to proselytize about the joys of exophony if they have never been forced to speak in a language not their own."

Tawada's irreverence for borders is not mere cosmopolitanism; she recognizes the way language always arrives to us from somewhere, and comes embedded in systems of power not of our choosing. Not all exophonic writers arrive at this conclusion, let alone have the ability to hold the weight and violence of language alongside its capacity for experimentation and play. We are so lucky that Yoko Tawada can do it all.

LISA HOFMANN-KURODA

Bringing a book from manuscript to what you are reading is a team effort.

Dialogue Books would like to thank everyone who helped to publish *Exophony* in the UK.

Editorial
Hannah Chukwu
Adriano Noble

Contracts
Stephanie Evans
Sasha Duszynska Lewis
Isabel Camara

Sales
Megan Schaffer
Kyla Dean
Dominic Smith
Sinead White
Georgina Cutler-Ross
Kerri Hood
Jess Harvey
Natasha Weninger-Kong

Design
Sara Mahon
Sasha Egonu

Production
Amanda Jones

Publicity
Corinna Zifko

Marketing
Emily Moran

Operations
Rosie Stevens

Finance
Chris Vale
Jonathan Gant

Audio
Carrie Hutchison